VOLUME ONE HUNDRED AND THREE

ADVANCES IN
COMPUTERS

VOLUME ONE HUNDRED AND THREE

Advances in
COMPUTERS

Edited by

ATIF M. MEMON
College Park, MD, United States

AMSTERDAM • BOSTON • HEIDELBERG • LONDON
NEW YORK • OXFORD • PARIS • SAN DIEGO
SAN FRANCISCO • SINGAPORE • SYDNEY • TOKYO
Academic Press is an imprint of Elsevier

Academic Press is an imprint of Elsevier
50 Hampshire Street, 5th Floor, Cambridge, MA 02139, United States
525 B Street, Suite 1800, San Diego, CA 92101-4495, United States
The Boulevard, Langford Lane, Kidlington, Oxford OX5 1GB, United Kingdom
125 London Wall, London, EC2Y 5AS, United Kingdom

First edition 2016

Notices
Knowledge and best practice in this field are constantly changing. As new research and experience broaden our understanding, changes in research methods, professional practices, or medical treatment may become necessary.

Practitioners and researchers must always rely on their own experience and knowledge in evaluating and using any information, methods, compounds, or experiments described herein. In using such information or methods they should be mindful of their own safety and the safety of others, including parties for whom they have a professional responsibility.

To the fullest extent of the law, neither the Publisher nor the authors, contributors, or editors, assume any liability for any injury and/or damage to persons or property as a matter of products liability, negligence or otherwise, or from any use or operation of any methods, products, instructions, or ideas contained in the material herein.

ISBN: 978-0-12-809941-4
ISSN: 0065-2458

For information on all Academic Press publications
visit our website at https://www.elsevier.com/

  Working together to grow libraries in developing countries

www.elsevier.com • www.bookaid.org

Publisher: Zoe Kruze
Acquisition Editor: Zoe Kruze
Editorial Project Manager: Shellie Bryant
Production Project Manager: Surya Narayanan Jayachandran
Cover Designer: Greg Harris

Typeset by SPi Global, India

CONTENTS

PREFACE

This volume of *Advances in Computers* is the 103rd in this series. This series, which has been continuously published since 1960, presents in each volume four to seven chapters describing new developments in software, hardware, or uses of computers. I invite leaders in their respective fields of computing to contribute a chapter about recent advances.

Volume 103 focuses on four important topics. In Chapter 1, entitled "How elasticity property plays an important role in the cloud: a survey," Bikas *et al.* discuss how a cloud environment allows consumers to deploy and run their software applications on a sophisticated infrastructure that is owned and managed by a cloud provider (eg, Amazon Web Services, Microsoft Azure, and Google Cloud Platform). These cloud users acquire resources for their applications on demand and pay only for the consumed resources. In order to take this advantage of cloud computing, it is vital for a consumer to determine if the cloud infrastructure can rapidly change the type and quantity of resources allocated to an application in the cloud according to the application's demand. This property of the cloud is known as elasticity. Ideally, a cloud platform should be perfectly elastic, ie, the resources allocated to an application exactly match the demand. This allocation should occur as the load to the application increases, with no degradation of applications response time, and a consumer should pay only for the resources used by the application. However, in reality, clouds are not perfectly elastic. One reason for that is it is difficult to predict the elasticity requirements of a given application and its workload in advance, and optimally match resources with the applications needs. This chapter investigates the elasticity problem in the cloud, and explains why it is still a challenging problem to solve and consider what services current cloud service providers are offering to maintain the elasticity in the cloud. Finally, the chapter discusses research that can be used to improve elasticity in the cloud.

In Chapter 2 entitled "Input-sensitive profiling: a survey," Alourani *et al.* present a broad overview of input-sensitive profiling, which is an automated analysis technique that calculates the resource usages (eg, the memory and the CPU usage) by methods during program execution for different combinations of input values. In addition to enabling developers to estimate the time and space complexities of a program, input-sensitive profiling also allows developers to automatically detect bottlenecks during performance testing, where the performance of a program suddenly worsens for a particular combination of input parameter values. One of the important advantages of this profiling technique is to identify what methods consume more resources (eg, CPU and memory usages) for specific combinations of input values and pinpoint why these methods are responsible for intensive execution time. Hence, developers can understand and optimize performance problems in a program and they can predict how likely that a program might not scale with increasing the size of the input (eg, adding more users or a larger set of values for a given input parameter). Unfortunately, it is very difficult to identify specific input values from a large number of combinations that lead to performance degradation of programs. This chapter explores the input-sensitive profiling problem and discusses its challenges. Some recent contributions of input-sensitive profiling algorithms that were developed to detect performance bottlenecks of a program are investigated and summarized.

Chapter 3, entitled "Recent advances in regression testing techniques," by Do covers the space of software systems and their environments that change continuously. They are enhanced, corrected, and ported to new platforms. These changes can affect a system adversely; thus software engineers perform regression testing to ensure the quality of the modified systems. Regression testing is an integral part of most major software projects, but as projects grow larger and the number of tests increases, performing regression testing becomes more expensive. To address this problem, many researchers and practitioners have proposed and empirically evaluated various regression testing techniques, such as regression test selection, test case prioritization, and test suite minimization. Recent surveys on these techniques indicate that this research area continues to grow, heuristics and the types of data utilized become diverse, and wider application domains have been considered. This chapter presents the current status and the trends of three regression testing techniques, and discusses recent advances of each technique.

Finally, Chapter 4, entitled "Coverage-based Software Testing: Beyond Basic Test Requirements," by Masri and Zaraket posits that code coverage is one of the core quality metrics adopted by software testing practitioners nowadays. Researchers have devised several coverage criteria that testers use to assess the quality of test suites. A coverage criterion operates by first defining a set of test requirements that need to be satisfied by the given test suite, and second, computing the percentage of the satisfied requirements, thus yielding a quality metric that quantifies the potential adequacy of the test suite at revealing program defects. What differentiates one coverage criterion from another is the set of test requirements involved. For example, function coverage is concerned with whether every function in the program has been called, and statement coverage is concerned with whether every statement in the program has been executed. The use of code coverage in testing is not restricted to assessing the quality of test suites. For example, researchers have devised test suite minimization and test case generation techniques that also leverage coverage. Early coverage-based software testing techniques involved basic test requirements such as functions, statements, branches, and predicates, whereas recent techniques involved test requirements that are complex code constructs such as paths, program dependences, and information flows; or test requirements that are not necessarily code constructs such as program properties, and user-defined test requirements. The focus of this chapter is to compare these two generations of techniques with regard to their effectiveness at revealing defects. The chapter first presents preliminary background and definitions and then describes impactful early coverage techniques followed by select recent work.

I hope that you find these articles of interest. If you have any suggestions of topics for future chapters, or if you wish to be considered as an author for a chapter, I can be reached at atif@cs.umd.edu.

Prof. ATIF M. MEMON, Ph.D.
College Park, MD, United States

CHAPTER ONE

How Elasticity Property Plays an Important Role in the Cloud: A Survey

M.A.N. Bikas, A. Alourani, M. Grechanik
University of Illinois at Chicago, Chicago, IL, United States

Contents

Abstract

In a cloud environment, consumers can deploy and run their software applications on a sophisticated infrastructure that is owned and managed by a cloud provider (eg, Amazon Web Services, Microsoft Azure, and Google Cloud Platform). Cloud users

1

can acquire resources for their applications on demand, and they have to pay only for the consumed resources. In order to take this advantage of cloud computing, it is vital for a consumer to determine if the cloud infrastructure can rapidly change the type and quantity of resources allocated to an application in the cloud according to the application's demand. This property of the cloud is known as elasticity. Ideally, a cloud platform should be perfectly elastic; ie, the resources allocated to an application exactly match the demand. This allocation should occur as the load to the application increases, with no degradation of application's response time, and a consumer should pay only for the resources used by the application. However, in reality, clouds are not perfectly elastic. One reason for that is it is difficult to predict the elasticity requirements of a given application and its workload in advance, and optimally match resources with the applications' needs. In this chapter, we investigate the elasticity problem in the cloud. We explain why it is still a challenging problem to solve and consider what services current cloud service providers are offering to maintain the elasticity in the cloud. Finally, we discuss the existing research that can be used to improve elasticity in the cloud.

1. INTRODUCTION

In recent years, cloud computing is receiving a great deal of attention in the industry and academic worlds. The primary motivation for companies to consider cloud platforms for their applications is the possibility of acquiring resources on demand and paying only for the resources used by the application. To understand the benefits of cloud computing, consider a scenario where a start-up company wants to launch a new service on the web. One of the approaches that the company can go with is the traditional infrastructure, which the company must purchase or build, and manage. With the traditional infrastructure approach, the company's engineers have to estimate the amount of hardware and the number of customers, and based on these estimations, the company will start providing the service with a required level of quality. Then, the employees of the company will buy or rent the hardware, install the necessary applications, and start providing the service. But the number of customers is often difficult to predict, and it changes significantly over time (eg, the company released a new feature that has become popular in just an hour and can multiply the number of users in a short time period). To handle this situation, the employees can acquire more hardware by paying additional costs; otherwise their estimated hardware will not be sufficient to provide the expected quality of the service and eventually will discourage potential customers. The problem with this approach is that the company will either end up paying a lot more than necessary or will lose customers.

Cloud computing platforms offer a solution to the above problem. In cloud computing, the company can deploy their software services at the cloud platform that is managed and owned by a cloud provider. With a cloud provider, the company can get resources for their services on demand and only pays for the resources that are actually used. The cloud provider typically runs large data centers with thousands of servers and hence can pay lower prices for the hardware and lower maintenance costs. According to Armbrust et al. [1], for a medium-sized data center, saving on costs can be of factor 5–7. Another advantage of cloud computing is the elasticity it can provide to software applications; ie, new resources can be allocated and assigned to a customer quickly. In the cloud, new resources will be allocated when the number of users increases and later resources will be released when they are not required anymore. This way, the company can save money by not paying for unnecessary infrastructure and can prevent degrading the quality of the service.

This chapter is organized as follows: Section 2 presents a cloud elasticity overview, the importance of the elasticity problem in the cloud, and how we can measure elasticity in the cloud. Section 3 presents the elasticity solutions and details what services existing cloud service providers are currently offering. Existing research issues of cloud elasticity are discussed in Section 4. Section 5 analyzes the existing works that can be utilized to improve the elasticity in the cloud and, finally, we conclude in Section 6.

2. CLOUD ELASTICITY

In cloud computing, resources can be dynamically provisioned on demand, and a customer has to pay only for the consumed resources. According to Mell et al. [2], these resources can be obtained quickly and in certain cases automatically to meet the workload change. For cloud consumers, the resources available for provisioning often appear to be infinite and can be acquired in any quantity at any time, at least in theory. Elasticity is often used interchangeably with scalability [3], but there are some differences. Scalability [3] is the ability of a system to sustain an increasing workload by adding more computing resources to maintain adequate performance, while elasticity is related to how well the system is dynamically provisioning resources according to the workload at any point in time. Elasticity considers both the growth and the reduction of the pool of cloud resources based on the demand, while scalability only considers the growth. As mentioned by Islam et al. [3], scalability does not consider how long it will take for the system to accomplish the required level of performance, whereas time is the central aspect of elasticity that depends on how quickly the system responds to a changed workload. This interplay between elasticity and scalability is important for evaluating the combined performance of applications that are deployed in the cloud.

In the subsequent sections, we cite some of the most commonly used definitions of cloud elasticity. Then, we will discuss the importance of elasticity property in the cloud and how elasticity can be measured in the cloud.

2.1 Elasticity Definitions

There are many works that try to define cloud computing elasticity. Despite that, there is no precise and common understanding of the term elasticity in the context of cloud computing. Nothing has been proposed so far to quantify and compare elasticity properties of different cloud service providers [4]. Here, we list some of the commonly used definitions of cloud elasticity to get the perspective about different usages of this term.

NIST defines cloud elasticity as [2]: "Rapid elasticity: Capabilities can be elastically provisioned and released, in some cases automatically, to scale rapidly outward and inward commensurate with demand. To the consumer, the capabilities available for provisioning often appear to be unlimited and can be appropriated in any quantity at any time."

Herbst *et al.* [4]: "Elasticity is the degree to which a system is able to adapt to workload changes by (de)allocating resources in an autonomic manner, such that at each point in time the available resources match the current demand as closely as possible."

Han *et al.* [5]: "Ability of the system to adaptively scale resources up and down in order to meet varying application demand."

Li *et al.* [6]: "How quickly a system can adapt to changes in the workload that may happen in a short amount of time."

Garg *et al.* [7]: "How much a cloud service can be scaled up and down during the peak times."

Perez-Sorrosal *et al.* [8]: "Capacity at runtime by adding and removing virtual resources without service interruption in order to handle variation in the workload."

Edwin Schouten, IBM, Thoughts on Cloud [9]: "Elasticity is essentially a rename of scalability. Scalability is the ability to add or remove capacity, mostly processing, memory, or both, to or from an IT environment when this is needed."

We define elasticity as the ability of a system to dynamically adjust virtual resources assigned to an application based on workload, and the allocated resources have to precisely match the demand as fast as the load to the application increases or decreases while maintaining the service-level agreements, and a consumer pays only for the resources used by the application.

2.2 Importance of Elasticity in the Cloud

Ideally, a cloud platform should be perfectly elastic; ie, the resources allocated to an application exactly match the demand, and this should happen as fast as the load increases with no degradation of the application's response time, and a consumer only pays for the resources used by the application. To host an application with a strict response time requirement and unpredictable workload, an elastic cloud would be an ideal platform [10]. On a traditional infrastructure, these types of applications are difficult to host because the quantity of resources that is needed to provide a guaranteed quality of service (QoS) is not known in advance. However, clouds are not perfectly elastic in reality because it is difficult to predict the elasticity requirements of a given application and its workload in advance and optimally match resources with the applications' needs. Moreover, there is a delay between the requested time of the resources and the availability of the resources to be used by the application [10]. The cloud infrastructure is not able to immediately respond to the application's demand because it should first look for an available server to create a new virtual machine instance and deploy the application, start the application, and include the newly added instance in a load balancer (eg, the Amazon Elastic Load Balancer) so that it can be accessed externally. The time required for all these steps is often referred to as the start-up time [10]. In practice, this start-up time depends on the particular cloud provider. The objective of cloud elasticity is to maximize the performance of applications hosted in the cloud by minimizing cost while maintaining the SLA requirements (eg, 90% of requests with less than 500 ms response time, 99.9% availability, etc.). To get the full advantage from a cloud system, we need proper elasticity solutions to achieve the elasticity objectives. Even though many elastic solutions have already been developed to minimize the elasticity problem in the cloud, still more work is required to manage cloud elasticity better.

2.3 How to Measure Elasticity

Different metrics are used to evaluate the elasticity in the cloud. Islam *et al.* [3] defined elasticity metrics based on the financial penalties imposed by cloud providers on cloud users by overprovisioning (ie, cloud users pay more than necessary for the resources to handle a workload) and underprovisioning (ie, cloud users face unacceptable latency due to unmet demand) of cloud resources. As proposed by the authors, to determine a single elasticity metric, cloud users should run different benchmark workloads on the cloud under investigation and take the geometric mean of the combined costs of overprovisioning and underprovisioning.

Garg *et al.* [7] proposed a metric for elasticity how a cloud service can be scaled up and down during peak intervals. They defined two attributes including mean time to expand and maximum capacity of the service that can be provided during peak periods. Bai *et al.* [11] proposed an elasticity metric based on the ratio of execution time over resource allocation like CPU and memory usage. Coutinho *et al.* [12] identified a list of elasticity metrics in their survey separated by different groups. The groups they used are resource allocation, capacity (resources and services availability), cost (financial cost or operational cost), QoS (service-level agreements), resource utilization (ie, resource demand, idleness, overutilization, and underutilization), scalability of the system, and time. Defining standard metrics for the measurement of cloud elasticity is not an easy task. Common metrics that can be used to measure elasticity are resource utilization, response time, throughput, scalability, availability, and reliability [12]. Among these metrics, resource utilization (eg, percentage of CPU allocation) is used by most of the current public cloud providers (eg, Amazon EC2, Azure). The performance of the application, for example, its throughput (expressed in the number of requests per second), is another frequently used elasticity metrics after resource utilization. The cost and pricing also play a very significant role in cloud elasticity. They are often associated with public cloud providers due to the nature of their resource acquisition, and each provider has a strategy to allocate resources [12]. Scalability is also identified by many as a strategy to provide elasticity. The performance of cloud elasticity depends on how long it takes to allocate and deallocate resources to an application based on demand. During the resource allocation time, the application's service will be interrupted, which is completely undesirable. We are still a long way from providing a desirable elasticity in the cloud. It is required to have some standard metrics that would be used by all cloud service provider to help their consumers to measure and compare cloud elasticity.

3. EXISTING CLOUD ELASTICITY SOLUTIONS

One of the biggest promises of cloud computing platforms is to support elasticity, which means on-demand allocation of resources to the applications based on workload. Resource allocation needs to be done in a cost-efficient manner while maintaining the quality of the services to the applications. Software engineers define how to deprovision resources for applications that are deployed in the cloud. Engineers study application behavior during software testing to maintain a particular performance. Based on that, they manually create efficient provisioning strategies (eg, if CPU usage is greater than 80%, then add one VM), which guide the cloud to scale the application's resources up or down. This engineering effort should also be minimized from the elasticity process. Currently, there are different solutions available that are being used by the cloud service providers to achieve elasticity. In the subsequent sections, we will analyze these solutions and discuss how these solutions work in the cloud to maintain the elasticity. Then, we will describe how some of the popular cloud service providers are offering their elasticity solution.

3.1 Classification of Cloud Elasticity Solutions

There are different elasticity solutions that exist in the cloud. These solutions can be classified in several categories based on different characteristics. As discussed in Refs. [12–14], elasticity solutions can be classified into reactive and predictive, based on the solution type. Based on the implementation techniques, it is possible to classify each type of elasticity solutions as Horizontal Scaling, Vertical Scaling, and Migration [13].

3.1.1 Reactive Elasticity Solution

Reactive elasticity solution reacts to the current load of the application to trigger some auto-scaling actions based on the given thresholds conditions (eg, resource utilization or violations of SLA). The reactive solution works based on the Rule-Condition-Action technique [13]. In a reactive solution, application owners manually provide auto-scaling rules that specify the threshold conditions for both provisioning and deprovisioning. An auto-scaling rule is composed of a set of threshold conditions and what scaling actions to be taken by the underlying cloud platform when any of the conditions is triggered. Every condition consists of one or more auto-scaling metrics, eg, CPU utilization or RAM usage, which are compared against a threshold or violations of SLA. Most of the cloud service providers provide these auto-scaling metrics through a monitoring service, for example, Amazon CloudWatch [15] monitoring service includes CPU usage, network traffic, disk reads, and writes. One of the auto-scaling rules for provisioning resources can be as follows: Condition (if CPU usage is greater than 85% for five consecutive minutes) and then Action (add one VM). The elasticity controller of underlying cloud platform continuously monitors these rules, and when one of these conditions is met, it triggers the appropriate scaling action [16].

The reactive solution is the most commonly used cloud elasticity solution and offered by popular cloud service providers such as Amazon [17], Microsoft Azure [18], and Google Cloud Platform (GCP) [19]. Several academic works [20–23] suggested some improvement over the rule-based reactive elasticity solution. For instance, Breitgand et al. [20] proposed an adaptive threshold-based algorithm using linear regression model, where the model recomputes new threshold values each time any of the predefined performance parameters is violated. However, threshold-based solutions adjust new threshold values only relying on the current system behavior and also require some historical data that might not be available every time.

3.1.2 Predictive Elasticity Solution

Unlike reactive solution, a predictive solution attempts to predict the future demand for an application to allocate sufficient resources in advance of the load. Predictive solutions use various analytical techniques (ie, time series analysis, queuing theory, control theory, or reinforcement learning) and different heuristics to determine when and how to (de)provision resources. One predictive policy can be to use a workload predictor to anticipate the future system load behavior from the history of the previous workloads, and then use a performance model to decide the quantity of resources (eg, number of VMs) required to service the anticipated load [24].

Various predictive solutions have been proposed to automatically scale resources. For example, Nguyen et al. [25] proposed an elastic resource scaling system using a wavelet-based [26] approach to predict the future resource needs of a cloud application for various workloads. A comprehensive analysis of predictive elasticity solution is presented in Section 5.4.

Hybrid elasticity solutions, combining both reactive and predictive solutions, have also been proposed by researchers (eg, Refs. [27–29]) to handle the inaccuracy in workload prediction. For example, Ali-Eldin *et al.* [28] proposed a hybrid solution based on queuing theory, where the authors used a reactive approach for scaling out and proactive for scaling in.

3.1.3 Horizontal Scaling

Horizontal scaling means adding or removing new instances (eg, VMs) to adapt to the changes in request load [16]. For example, add a new VM when the load increases and remove a VM when the load decreases. This technique is also called replication as a new replica of the same instance is being created to handle the increased user load. To distribute the load between different replicas, cloud platforms offer a load-balancing feature (eg, Amazon Elastic Load Balancer). Most of the current cloud service providers, for example, Amazon Web Services [17], use the horizontal scaling technique to provide elasticity.

3.1.4 Vertical Scaling

Vertical scaling means adding or removing resources (eg, CPU, memory) to an already running instance (eg, VM) on the fly, without restarting the instance [16]. For example, adding more CPU or memory to an already running virtual machine. This can also be referred to as the *hot-add feature* in the cloud. Most common operating systems do not support making any changes to their resources (eg, CPU, memory) on the fly without a reboot [16]. For this reason, current cloud providers do not offer this vertical scaling elasticity. Public cloud providers are trying to mimic this on-the-fly vertical scaling technique, by replacing a more powerful VM for a less powerful one. For example, AWS allows its users to change the instance type based on the load; however, a reboot of the instance is necessary, and this could take several minutes.

3.1.5 Migration

Migration means transferring a running instance (eg, VM) from a physical server to another physical server to handle the increase/decrease in application workload. The migration technique can be used as an alternative to vertical scaling, where an application is migrated to a larger capacity VM to keep up the growth in workload [13]. However, during the migration process, application service might be interrupted, and hence, performance of the application is likely to be affected. Many cloud providers (eg, Amazon Web Services) presently do not support live migration. However, VMware vSphere [30] supports live migration of an entire running VM from one server to another server without having to shut it down.

3.2 How Current Cloud Service Providers Are Offering Elasticity

This section presents an overview of how current cloud service providers are offering elasticity solutions.

Amazon Web Services [17] is one of the leading cloud service providers. AWS provides its elasticity solution using a replication technique called Auto-scaling [31] as part of their EC2 service offering. Auto-scaling solution works based on a concept of auto-scaling groups, where a customer has to specify a minimum and a maximum number of EC2 instances in each auto-scaling group to handle the load for their application. Auto-scaling uses a reactive approach where the customer also has to specify a set of auto-scaling rules (eg, if CPU usage exceeds 80%, then add a VM) that determines the number of VMs to be added or removed when the demand on the application increases or decreases. Amazon CloudWatch [15] monitoring service provides the metric values to help the customers to determine auto-scaling rules, which includes CPU usage, network traffic, disk read, and writes. APIs and a command-line interface can also be used for manually accessing the scaling features. Additionally, the solution includes an external elastic load balancer for distributing the workload to active EC2 instances. The auto-scaling architecture is illustrated in Fig. 1. As it can be seen, to use

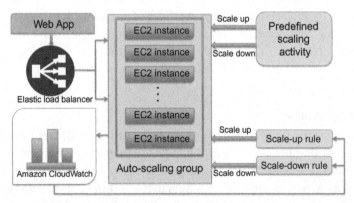

Fig. 1 How AWS offers elasticity. *Adapted from H. Ganesan, Auto-scaling Using AWS. http://www.slideshare.net/harishganesan/auto-scaling-using-amazon-web-services-aws, November 2015.*

the auto-scaling solution efficiently, customers have to come up with at least two rules to determine when to scale out and scale in. Amazon uses only the horizontal scaling technique to provide elasticity. Amazon presently does not support vertical scaling or migration. However, it allows the users to change the EC2 instance type, depending on the load, but for that a reboot is necessary, and this process can take up to several minutes.

Microsoft Azure [18] offers both Platform as a Service (PaaS) and Infrastructure as a Service (IaaS). With Azure IaaS, users can host their application either in a VM, where they are responsible for managing everything, or by installing the OS to make up the application running on it. And with Azure PaaS, users can host their application using Azure Cloud Service, where users can create either a web role (a web role is a front-end instance configured to run web applications supported by IIS, such as ASP.NET, and PHP) or a worker role (a worker role is a backbend instance configured to run applications and services-level tasks that do not require IIS) [32]. Like Amazon, Azure also uses a reactive approach, where the users have to specify a set of auto-scaling metrics. Azure presently uses only horizontal scaling techniques. To automatically scale an application running either on VMs, web roles or worker roles, users have to set some metrics in the Azure Management Portal. The auto-scaling metrics currently provided by the Azure through portal are Average CPU usage and Queue message [33]. One of the auto-scaling rules in Azure can be, if CPU usage >75%, to add a new web role instance. The Azure Watch, [34] which is being replaced with Cloudmonix [35], developed by Paraleap, provides an elasticity service to monitor and auto-scale any Azure-based solutions. Azure Watch offers an elasticity service by inspecting the performance of Azure-based applications, and based on that, they automatically allocate resources for the applications according to real-time workload.

GCP [19] also implements reactive horizontal elasticity like AWS and Azure. Google Cloud provides elasticity through a managed instance group, where a user can create and manage virtual machine instances. Google allows a maximum of 500 instances in a single managed instance group [36]. Then, the user has to create an autoscaler with an auto-scaling policy, where the autoscaler uses the defined policy to scale in or scale out. The currently supported auto-scaling policies by GCP are average CPU utilization, cloud monitoring metrics, and request per second. For example, if we define an auto-scaling policy as "0.85 average CPU utilization," then the autoscaler will try to maintain 85% CPU usage among all the cores in the instance group virtual machines. The autoscaler will automatically add more instances (user-specified) to the instance group if the average usage of the total cores goes beyond the target utilization and will remove instances otherwise. Google also offers APIs that can be used to set custom auto-scaling policies and to manage resources in the managed instance group. Google Compute Engine also provides a load-balancing service to distribute incoming network traffic across multiple virtual machine instances in the managed instance group.

Similarly, VMware [37], IBM [38], and Rackspace [39] as well as many other cloud providers also offer the rule-based reactive elasticity services through a managed control panel and APIs. RightScale [40] and Scalr [41] are two popular cloud management platforms that sit on top of various cloud providers (ie, AWS [17], GoGrid [42], etc.) and provide services to monitor and manage the elasticity of the underlying clouds.

4. EXISTING RESEARCH ISSUES OF CLOUD ELASTICITY

Cloud providers and academic researchers developed numerous elasticity solutions. However, there are still some existing cloud elasticity issues need to be adequately addressed. In this section, we describe the major challenges related to cloud elasticity.

4.1 Resource Availability

Cloud computing provides the illusion of unlimited resources available on demand. However, public cloud providers violate the promise of unlimited resources by determining a fixed number of computing resources that can be acquired by each user at any time [13]. For example, Amazon EC2 enables users to allocate 20 simultaneous instances on demand and 100 instances per region at the same time [13]. Rackspace provides a maximum limit of 65 GB of total memory for all users or 130 servers with 512 MB of memory per region [14]. For the majority of application owners, the quota allowed by the cloud providers is sufficient for their applications. However, if highly scalable resource-intensive applications (eg, pattern matching) start to use cloud computing effectively, these applications may shortly reach the scaling limits assumed for resource availability [13].

4.2 Interoperability Between Clouds

The use of different clouds to meet the needed of resources is one of the solutions to the resource availability issue. However, using various public clouds together remains challenging because of the lack of interoperability and portability between the clouds that caused by the limitation of standardized APIs [13]. Also, each cloud provider has its way of how cloud users and applications interact with the cloud [43]. For this reason, the migration of virtual machines among clouds and the communication between applications in different clouds is a very difficult task. To produce a huge-scale elastic computing models by combining different clouds, an evaluation toward a standardized API is a must. Some initiatives are going on to create global cloud standards. For example, the Cloud Computing Interoperability Forum (CCIF) [44] is working to create an open and standardized cloud framework that allows multiple cloud platforms to exchange information in a unified way. IEEE also has a similar project called Guide for Cloud Portability and Interoperability [45].

4.3 Resources Granularity Problem

Currently, most cloud service providers offer virtual machines as scaling units (eg, instance types in the Amazon EC2). However, resources should be available to users at any granularity that allows users to allocate different amounts of I/O resources and memory dynamically in a fine-grained fashion [14]. Also, acquiring a fixed combination of cloud resources cannot match the applications' demands and does not reflect the interests of users [46]. Another problem is that most of the cloud providers do not support vertical elasticity, which means it is not possible to add resources (eg, CPU, memory) to a running virtual machine (or instance) [12]. Many cloud service providers started offering vertical scaling of resources. For example, GoGrid [42] allows its user to increase memory vertically, and Amazon allows changing the instance type. However, VM rebooting is required, which yields several additional minutes.

4.4 Start-Up Time Problem

One of the important advantages of the elasticity is the capability to dynamically deprovision resources according to demand. On the other hand, one potential problem with this dynamic provisioning process is that it takes time. In addition to unpredictable changes in workload, it lacks the ability to provision resources in advance. Start-up time represents the length of time between requesting and acquiring resources that are available for use by cloud consumers [10]. The start-up time may take up to 10 min, which is affected by multiple factors, including the type of cloud platform, data center location, VM type, available resources in a region, image size, and the number of VMs [10]. Thus, if a cloud platform does not allocate required resources in a timely fashion, it could result in the underprovisioning of resources, which will adversely affect applications performance. Mao et al. [47] did a performance study on VM start-up time by comparing three different cloud providers—Amazon EC2, Windows Azure, and Rackspace. Their study shows that EC2 instance start-up time can be as high as 13 min, which is shown in Table 1.

On the opposite side, if a cloud platform does not release resources when an application no longer needs them, the application's owner could be over-charged for resource use. Amazon bills its customers on a per hour basis, which means that a customer has to pay for a full hour from the time the instance is allocated even though the instance might be deallocated immediately after being allocated [14]. Microsoft Azure bills its customers for a complete hour per each clock hour that an instance is deployed. For instance, if an Azure instance is allocated at 9:58 am and deallocated at 11:02 am, the customer is charged for 2 h [14].

4.5 Elasticity Requirement

Each application hosted in the cloud behaves differently. Different applications may require different resources to satisfy the same customer demands. It may be difficult, if not impossible, to match required resources with applications' needs optimally. Based on the halting problem [48], we can conclude that it is impossible to determine whether the program will finish

Table 1 Average VM Start-Up Time

Cloud	Operating System	Average VM Start-Up Time in Seconds
Azure	WebRole	374.8
Azure	WorkerRole	406.2
Azure	VMRole	356.6
Rackspace	Linux	44.2
Rackspace	Windows	429.2
EC2	Linux	96.9
EC2	Windows	810.2

Picture is taken from M. Mao, M. Humphrey, A performance study on the VM startup time in the cloud, in: IEEE 5th International Conference on Cloud Computing (CLOUD), June, IEEE, 2012, pp. 423–430.

running or continue running forever with a high degree of precision. To ensure proper elasticity, customer needs have to be considered while deploying applications in the cloud. One possible solution to meet elasticity requirements is to make an optimal trade-off between performance and cost. However, it is a difficult task due to the complexity of application behavior and the multiple dimensions of elasticity [49].

4.6 Automated Elasticity Mechanism

Elasticity solutions implemented by public cloud service providers are not fully automated. Application owners have to manually provide rules that specify the threshold conditions for both provisioning and deprovisioning. Every condition is composed of a series of auto-scaling metrics. These metrics include CPU usage, memory usage, I/O usage, the number of active connections, throughput, and latency. One of the conditions for provisioning resources can be that if CPU usage is greater than 80% for five consecutive minutes, then add one VM. The elasticity controller continuously monitors these conditions, and when one of these conditions is met, it triggers the appropriate scaling operation. Providing suitable threshold provisioning conditions for any specific application is a very tricky task, and in many cases, it could cause instability in the system. Additionally, fixed thresholds would be invalid as long as the application behavior is dynamic [12]. These conditions are appropriate for an application when the load can be anticipated or predicted to some extent. However, in a real-world scenario, it is very difficult, if not impossible, to predict the future load of a certain application. Therefore, it is important to tackle the different conditions of applications derived from the unanticipated workload by developing an automated and efficient auto-scaling approach. The automated elasticity problem can be addressed by using different approaches such as time series analysis, queuing theory, control theory, threshold-based policies, or reinforcement learning [12].

4.7 Oscillation Problem

In the cloud, when allocating resources for a software application, developers are liable to overprovision it (ie, allocating more resources than required, which results in the consumer's paying more than necessary), and an SLA violation occurs at the same time, and this is called the oscillation problem. For example, consider a scenario where the resource demands of an application are two CPUs and 2 GB of memory, and the cloud platform allocated five CPUs and 1 GB of memory to it. Thus, the consumer has to pay for three extra CPUs, but the application has unacceptable latency or timed out because of the unmet memory requirements, which caused the SLA violation. Oscillation problem is also illustrated in Fig. 2. Islam *et al.* [3] first observed this situation during their experiment with Amazon EC2. Later, Lorido-Botran *et al.* [50] mentioned about this problem in their review article. An oscillation problem can be caused by providing the improper type or quantity of resources to the application in the cloud. Another reason could be delays in providing the right resources and deprovisioning the unnecessary resources according to the application's workload. Oscillation problem does not only degrade applications' QoS but are also costly, making consumers pay for unnecessary resources.

4.8 Auto-Scaling Metrics and Benchmarking Tools

Different cloud providers use different auto-scaling metrics (eg, CPU utilization) in an isolated manner. For example, currently, Amazon EC2 [31] provides CPU utilization, memory utilization, the number of requests/second, and response time as scaling metrics, along with some other metrics. Azure [18] provides average CPU usage and queue messages as scaling metrics. It is very difficult for customers to understand which metrics they should use to properly provision their application hosted in the cloud.

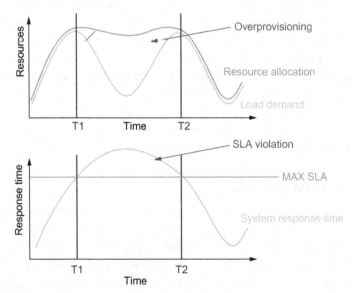

Fig. 2 Oscillation problem.

It is important to define metrics in such a way as to capture different aspects of elasticity. Besides, new benchmark tools are necessary to assess the elasticity of cloud environments properly.

5. HOW ELASTICITY CAN BE IMPROVED IN THE CLOUD

In this section, we discuss the existing works contributed toward the elasticity that can be used to improve the elasticity property in the cloud.

5.1 How to Maximize Resource Availability in the Cloud?

One of the main issues of cloud computing is the availability of resources in the cloud. Several factors should be addressed to ensure the high availability of the application on the cloud, including hardware and software failures, specifically single points of failures, network vulnerabilities, power outages, conservations, or denial of service invasions. An efficient deprovisioning of resource reduces the low availability of the services (eg, application) on the cloud. We summarize some of the solutions that address resource availability problem.

Armbrust et al. [1] discussed how availability is one of the top obstacles in cloud computing. Although the authors have analyzed the high-availability approaches used by cloud providers, they do not discuss any existing solutions that enable a cross-cloud resource provisioning model. Cloud providers (eg, GCP, Amazon Web Services, Microsoft Azure, GoGrid, and Rackspace) lack a common platform for cross-cloud provisioning.

Galante et al. [13] pointed out that the use of multiple clouds is one of the solutions to the resources availability issue. The CCIF [44] attempted to overcome the limitations of interoperability standards among various cloud platforms by introducing an open and standardized cloud interface to unify different cloud platform APIs. IEEE also has a similar project P2301 (Guide for Cloud Portability and Interoperability) [45], where the purpose of the project is to guide cloud users to develop and use cloud services using a common standard to increase portability and interoperability among different providers.

Buyya et al. [51] proposed architecture for cloud federation to integrate distributed clouds to meet business requirements. A federated cloud enables cloud providers to manage and deploy several external and internal cloud computing services. For example, it allows fulfilling the exceeding demands of a cloud by renting resources from other cloud service providers.

Pawluk *et al.* [52] developed an initial step toward the idea of a cloud of clouds [53] to enable an automated cross-cloud resource provisioning platform. They proposed a broker service that enables cross-cloud to facilitate the construction of application topology platform and runtime modification according to the objectives of an application deployer. In most cases, the assumption of acquired resources should be homogeneous. However, the authors eliminated this assumption to support an actual intercloud platform. An open project [54] for cross-cloud acquirement and VM management enables a developer to select which of the available clouds to use, whereas Pawluk *et al.* [52] select the available clouds to use for the developer.

An attempt to define unified access to multiple clouds via a unified API has been advanced by Refs. [44,45,54], whereas Refs. [51,52] introduced a methodology for the federation of cloud computing platforms. Both works do not discuss any implementation to automate the resource acquirement procedure via unified access to multiple clouds. References [44,45] presented limited support for interoperability and intercloud interfaces, but they did not provide any mechanism (eg, implementation) to automate the resource acquirement procedure via unified access to multiple clouds through APIs.

These studies have proposed solutions to the problems associated with resource availability of cloud systems. These solutions are very valuable to ensure the high availability of the services on the cloud systems to maintain elasticity.

5.2 How to Minimize the Resource Provisioning Time in the Cloud

One of the main concerns of cloud computing is resource provisioning time, the length of time between scaling up/down and actual resource provisioning/deprovisioning time. Although cloud users can acquire resources (eg, VM) at any time, it takes a while for the acquired VMs to be available for use. The duration of time, which is called the start-up time, is caused by the search for a spot for provisioning the VM in the data centers, including allocating IP address, configuring the OS, and booting the OS. Moreover, this start-up time is affected by multiple factors, including data center location, VM type, image size, and the number of VMs. Cloud providers support various resource provisioning times [10]. Cloud users are aware of the start-up time problem and complained about the need to improve the performance of their cloud applications [55,56]. The provisioning time should be taken into consideration while designing the control mechanism for elastic applications. For example, the elasticity time was taken by provisioning a new VM for a specific application component. We discuss some of the solutions that address resource provisioning time.

Multiple researchers measured the efficiency of start-up time using the overall performance of a cloud provider. For instance, Ostermann *et al.* [57] evaluated the different VM start-up times for one-instance and several-instance requests in EC2. Hill *et al.* [58] compared the VM start-up process between WebRole and WorkerRole in Microsoft Azure. Both works do not consider the new services (eg, VMRole of Azure [32] or spot instances of Amazon [59]) and other elements, such as the size of OS image, type of instance, location of a data center, and time of the day.

The need to speed up the start-up time has been advanced by Refs. [60–63]. Nguyen *et al.* [25] showed how dynamic VM cloning technique can be used to reduce the application start-up time so that new VMs will be ready before overloads occur. Wu *et al.* [60] also developed techniques based on VM cloning to accelerate the speed of cloud deployment. Zhu *et al.* [61] designed a fast start approach by taking a snapshot of the deployed VM that hosts the configured application. Tang *et al.* [62] developed a VM image called FVD to enable the migration and creation of instant VM. Peng *et al.* [63] introduced a chuck-level VM image technique for the distribution network to minimize the VM instance provisioning time by supporting collaboration sharing in cloud data centers. Villegas *et al.* [64] discussed changing providers billing policy and virtualization techniques to overcome the spin-up/down times. OSv [65] is a cloud-based operating system, which is designed for running only a single application on a VM. Even though it can boot within just a few second, it takes longer time to deprovision a VM.

In addition, other works [66–69] used spot instances to accelerate the speed of their job execution and reduce their job execution cost. In these works, the cost of spot instances was assumed to be cheaper than that of on-demand instances. Cloud customers receive higher computing power for spot instances than for on-demand instances. On the other hand, these techniques do not observe the longer VM start-up time.

We review the recent studies related to the resource provisioning time in order to understand how to improve the performance of software applications that are hosted in the cloud environment.

5.3 How to Minimize the Resource Provisioning Cost in the Cloud?

Cloud computing has grown to support the demands of big data by developing a pay-as-you-go cost model that allows users to minimize the cost of rented resources and to maintain QoS (eg, throughput, reliability, availability, security, response time, and performance). The resource provisioning cost, which represents the cost of utilizing computing resources (eg, RAM, CPU, and VM), is one of the main concerns of cloud computing. It is difficult to apply perfectly the pay-as-you-go cost model due to the difficulty of allocating the right quantity of resources required for the execution of an application. To improve the elasticity in the cloud, resource provisioning cost should be minimized. We have summarized some of the solutions that address how resource provisioning cost can be minimized.

Amazon [59] offers an elasticity solution based on cost called Spot Instances. Spot Price determines the hourly cost of using virtual servers via an auction by gathering user bids and estimating available capacity. The user request of instances is fulfilled once his or her bid exceeds the current Spot Price. These instances are kept allocated unless the user terminates them or the current Spot Price exceeds the user bid. The provision of spot instances has been advanced by Refs. [66,69,70]. In Ref. [66], the checkpointing technique was developed to minimize the cost of resource provisioning and to maintain the availability of spot instances. Andrzejak et al. [70] consider a probabilistic algorithm that enables cloud users to bid prices for spot instances efficiently.

Yu et al. [71] introduced a cost-efficient database placement algorithm by combining a migration plan to minimize the migration cost and a reactive solution to maximize the cloud resource usage. Authors create a migration plan based on user and system preferences (eg, resource constraints) along with generating a detailed database placement. Their case study was evaluated on top of an IBM cloud platform.

Sharma et al. [27] proposed a system that reduces cloud deployment cost and is elastic to workload changes by taking into consideration each VM instance cost, the opportunities of replicating or migrating the VM, and transformation time from one configuration to another. Hence, this system provides the minimum cost configuration in linear time.

Brebner [10] proposed a fine-grained cost model to charge for consumed resources such as the stored byte, the transmitted byte, and the time unit (eg, millisecond) of processing.

Hong et al. [72] presented work on a vision of an optimal margin cost at the same time, guaranteeing statistical response time. Chaisiri et al. [73] introduced multiple virtual server provisioning techniques to reduce the cost of provisioning for different term planning, using reliable optimization, complex programming, and average sampling approximation techniques.

On the other hand, these works only consider cost optimization rather than time-cost trade-offs. The time-cost trade-offs problem has been addressed in Ref. [74] by proposing an optimized algorithm to deal with processing time and monetary costs in the context of the cloud.

In addition, the provision of reserved instances has been investigated in Refs. [75,76]. In Refs. [75,76], complex programming was used to solve uncertainties and to improve the reserved resource numbers for long terms.

We analyze some recent contributions toward the resource provisioning cost in the cloud. It is vital to provision virtual resources precisely and automatically in the cloud for maintaining a certain performance for software applications by providing required resources that satisfy pay-as-you-go cost model.

5.4 How to Predict Future Resource Demand in Cloud?

One of the biggest concerns of cloud elasticity is predicting the future resource demand of applications to deal with the changes in workload. To do this proactively, cloud system providers or application owners need to know exactly when to start allocating resources (eg, VMs) for an application and, more importantly, how many resources (eg, the number of VMs) to allocate. The unpredictable nature of workload, a lack of detailed knowledge about the application, and multitenancy make the demand prediction so difficult in the cloud [25]. Presently, cloud providers reactively allocate resources based on the user-defined rules, for example, Amazon EC2 Auto-scaling [31], that specify when to add or release resources to deal with load changes. As a result of this inaccurate resource prediction, cloud users may either pay more than necessary because of the over-allocation of resources or lose their potential customers due to the missing SLAs. Here, we discuss some of the recent works that addresses the resource demand prediction problem in the cloud that can be used to improve elasticity.

Nguyen et al. [25] proposed a wavelet-based distributed resource scaling system called AGILE to predict the resource demand of a multitier cloud application in advance. Based on the predicted demand, they described a model to determine the quantity of resources using online profiling and polynomial curve fitting for maintaining the application's performance.

Gong et al. [77] proposed an elasticity system coined PRESS by using signal processing techniques to predict online future resource demand in the cloud. The authors used a statistical state-driven learning algorithm to perform the short-term resource prediction and used a discrete-time Markov chain model to do the long-term prediction.

CloudScale [78] is a predictive resource scaling system, which is a successor of Press [77] that performs online prediction of resource demand (eg, CPU usage of VMs) without any prior knowledge about the application. CloudScale mainly gives emphasis on minimizing the prediction error, unlike Press, which focuses on achieving high prediction accuracy.

LaCurts *et al.* [79] proposed a framework to predict the future network bandwidth for applications hosted in a cloud data center by analyzing the tenant's past network usage.

Some of the early works, for example, Shen *et al.* [80] and Chandra *et al.* [81], proposed resource prediction algorithms by observing previous application workload and corresponding response times using Auto Regression techniques to allocate resources dynamically within a single server.

Gmach *et al.* [82] used an FFT-based technique to perform a long-term workload prediction. Vasić *et al.* [83] proposed a predictive framework, which used online clustering based on the history of the VMs to cope with various loads. Similarly, Refs. [84–89] used various time series prediction algorithms to achieve resource demand prediction in the cloud.

The predictive solutions mentioned earlier mainly used a time series analysis mechanism that tries to find the repeating pattern in the future workload based on the previous demand history. This is one of the most popular techniques to predict future resource demand in the cloud. However, the accuracy of these solutions heavily depends on choosing an appropriate time series prediction algorithm (ie, Moving Average, Auto Regression, ARMA (Auto Regression-Moving Average), Support Vector Machine, Support Vector Regression, Neural Networking Models, Pattern matching, Signal Processing Techniques, etc.), length of the demand history, and the prediction interval [50].

Many predictive elasticity solutions [90–100] used control theory to adaptively perform prediction of future demand for resources based on various performance models, such as Kalman filter, Smoothing splines, and Fuzzy model. However, the prediction accuracy of those solutions highly depends on the efficient design of the controllers [50].

Also, many works [5,101–112] have extensively studied queuing theory to determine how resources (eg, VMs) are required in each tier to handle varying application workloads. However, those solutions can create significant overheads to the underlying cloud systems, and a certain level of prior application knowledge is required to build an effective predictive model [78].

Lorido-Botran *et al.* [50] conducted an interesting survey on auto-scaling techniques, where the authors classified many predictive elasticity solutions based on various forecasting models, such as time series analysis, queuing theory, control theory or reinforcement learning, and static threshold-based rules.

So many studies about predictive solutions give a clear idea of how important it is in the cloud to anticipate future demand for the applications based on the load variations. These solutions are undoubtedly a step forward toward achieving a perfect elastic environment in the cloud.

6. CONCLUSION

The objective of this survey paper is to present a comprehensive study to show how elasticity property plays an important role in the cloud. In addition, this paper helps to better understand the concept of cloud elasticity and motivates to develop new solutions. Initially, we described an overview of cloud elasticity. We discussed the cloud elasticity solutions and how the cloud providers are offering elasticity. We analyzed the current research issues of cloud elasticity and existing works that can be utilized to improve elasticity in the cloud. Despite the vast amount of research related to cloud elasticity, researchers still have many arising challenges to tackle to achieve a perfectly elastic solution in the cloud.

REFERENCES

[1] M. Armbrust, A. Fox, R. Griffith, A.D. Joseph, R. Katz, A. Konwinski, et al., A view of cloud computing, Commun. ACM 53 (4) (2010) 50–58.

[2] P. Mell, T. Grance, The NIST Definition of Cloud Computing, National Institute of Standards and Technology, Gaithersburg, MD, 2011. http://nvlpubs.nist.gov/nistpubs/Legacy/SP/nistspecialpublication800-145.pdf.

[3] S. Islam, K. Lee, A. Fekete, A. Liu, How a consumer can measure elasticity for cloud platforms, in: Proceedings of the 3rd ACM/SPEC International Conference on Performance Engineering, ACM, Boston, MA, April 2012, pp. 85–96.

[4] N.R. Herbst, S. Kounev, R. Reussner, Elasticity in cloud computing: what it is, and what it is not, in: Proceedings of the 10th International Conference on Autonomic Computing (ICAC), San Jose, CA, June 2013, pp. 23–27.

[5] R. Han, M.M. Ghanem, L. Guo, Y. Guo, M. Osmond, Enabling cost-aware and adaptive elasticity of multi-tier cloud applications, Future Gener. Comput. Syst. 32 (2014) 82–98.

[6] M. Li, F. Ye, M. Kim, H. Chen, H. Lei, A scalable and elastic publish/subscribe service, in: IEEE International Symposium on Parallel and Distributed Processing (IPDPS), IEEE, May 2011, pp. 1254–1265.

[7] S.K. Garg, S. Versteeg, R. Buyya, A framework for ranking of cloud computing services, Future Gener. Comput. Syst. 29 (4) (2013) 1012–1023.

[8] F. Perez-Sorrosal, M. Patiño-Martinez, R. Jimenez-Peris, B. Kemme, Elastic SI-Cache: consistent and scalable caching in multi-tier architectures, VLDB J. 20 (6) (2011) 841–865.

[9] E. Schouten, Rapid Elasticity and the Cloud, http://www.thoughtsoncloud.com/2012/09/rapid-elasticity-and-the-cloud, 2015. November.

[10] P.C. Brebner, Is your cloud elastic enough?: performance modelling the elasticity of infrastructure as a service (IaaS) cloud applications, in: Proceedings of the 3rd ACM/SPEC International Conference on Performance Engineering, ACM, Boston, MA, April 2012, pp. 263–266.

[11] X. Bai, M. Li, B. Chen, W.T. Tsai, J. Gao, Cloud testing tools, in: IEEE 6th International Symposium on Service Oriented System Engineering (SOSE), 2011, 2011, pp. 1–12.

[12] E.F. Coutinho, F.R. de Carvalho Sousa, P.A.L. Rego, D.G. Gomes, J.N. de Souza, Elasticity in cloud computing: a survey, Ann. Telecommun. 70 (2015) 289–309.

[13] G. Galante, L.C.E. de Bona, A survey on cloud computing elasticity, in: IEEE Fifth International Conference on Utility and Cloud Computing (UCC), November 2012, pp. 263–270.

[14] G. Galante, L.C.E. De Bona, A.R. Mury, B. Schulze, Are public clouds elastic enough for scientific computing? in: A.R. Lomuscio, S. Nepal, F. Patrizi, B. Benatallah, I. Brandić (Eds.), Service-Oriented Computing—ICSOC 2013 Workshops, Springer International Publishing, Berlin, Germany, 2013, pp. 294–307.

[15] Amazon CloudWatch. http://aws.amazon.com/cloudwatch, November 2015.

[16] L.M. Vaquero, L. Rodero-Merino, R. Buyya, Dynamically scaling applications in the cloud, ACM SIGCOMM Comput. Commun. Rev. 41 (1) (2011) 45–52.

[17] Amazon Web Services. http://aws.amazon.com, November 2015.

[18] Microsoft Azure. https://azure.microsoft.com, November 2015.

[19] Google Cloud Platform. https://cloud.google.com, November 2015.

[20] D. Breitgand, E. Henis, O. Shehory, Automated and adaptive threshold setting: enabling technology for autonomy and self-management, in: Proceedings of IEEE Second International Conference on Autonomic Computing, ICAC, IEEE, Seattle, WA, June 2005, pp. 204–215.

[21] S. Meng, L. Liu, V. Soundararajan, Tide: achieving self-scaling in virtualized datacenter management middleware, in: Proceedings of the 11th International Middleware Conference Industrial Track, ACM, Bangalore, India, November 2010, pp. 17–22.

[22] P. Marshall, K. Keahey, T. Freeman, Elastic site: using clouds to elastically extend site resources, in: Proceedings of the 2010 10th IEEE/ACM International Conference on Cluster, Cloud and Grid Computing, IEEE Computer Society, Melbourne, Victoria, Australia, May 2010, pp. 43–52.

[23] R.N. Calheiros, C. Vecchiola, D. Karunamoorthy, R. Buyya, The Aneka platform and QoS-driven resource provisioning for elastic applications on hybrid clouds, Future Gener. Comput. Syst. 28 (6) (2012) 861–870.

[24] L.R. Moore, K. Bean, T. Ellahi, A coordinated reactive and predictive approach to cloud elasticity, Cloud Comput. 2013 (2013) 87–92.

[25] H. Nguyen, Z. Shen, X. Gu, S. Subbiah, J. Wilkes, Agile: elastic distributed resource scaling for infrastructure-as-a-service, in: Proceedings of the USENIX International Conference on Automated Computing (ICAC 2013). San Jose, CA, 2013.

[26] A.N. Akansu, R.A. Haddad, Multiresolution Signal Decomposition: Transforms, Subbands, and Wavelets, Academic Press, San Diego, CA, 2001.

[27] U. Sharma, P. Shenoy, S. Sahu, A. Shaikh, A cost-aware elasticity provisioning system for the cloud, in: Proceedings of the 31st International Conference on Distributed Computing Systems (ICDCS), IEEE, Minneapolis, MN, June 2011, pp. 559–570.

[28] A. Ali-Eldin, J. Tordsson, E. Elmroth, An adaptive hybrid elasticity controller for cloud infrastructures, in: IEEE Network Operations and Management Symposium (NOMS), IEEE, 2012, pp. 204–212.

[29] W. Iqbal, M.N. Dailey, D. Carrera, P. Janecek, Adaptive resource provisioning for read intensive multi-tier applications in the cloud, Future Gener. Comput. Syst. 27 (6) (2011) 871–879.

[30] VMware vSphere. https://www.vmware.com/products/vsphere/features/vmotion, November 2015.

[31] Amazon EC2 Auto-scaling. https://aws.amazon.com/autoscaling, November 2015.

[32] Microsoft Azure Service Offerings. https://azure.microsoft.com/en-us/documentation/articles/fundamentals-application-models, November 2015.

[33] Microsoft Azure Auto-scaling. https://azure.microsoft.com/en-us/documentation/articles/cloud-services-how-to-scale, November 2015.

[34] AzureWatch. https://www.paraleap.com/AzureWatch, November 2015.

[35] CloudMonix. http://cloudmonix.com, November 2015.

[36] Google Cloud Platform Instance Group. https://cloud.google.com/compute/docs/instance-groups, November 2015.

[37] VMware. http://www.vmware.com, November 2015.

[38] IBM Cloud. http://www.ibm.com/cloud-computing, November 2015.

[39] Rackspace Cloud. http://www.rackspace.com/cloud, November 2015.

[40] RightScale. http://www.rightscale.com, November 2015.

[41] Scalr. http://www.scalr.com, November 2015.

[42] GoGrid. https://www.datapipe.com/gogrid, November 2015.

[43] T. Dillon, C. Wu, E. Chang, Cloud computing: issues and challenges, in: Proceedings of the 24th IEEE International Conference on Advanced Information Networking and Applications (AINA), IEEE, Perth, Australia, April 2010, pp. 27–33.

[44] The Cloud Computing Interoperability Forum. http://www.cloudforum.org, November 2015.

[45] Guide for Cloud Portability and Interoperability Profiles. http://standards.ieee.org/develop/project/2301.html, November 2015.

[46] O. Agmon Ben-Yehuda, M. Ben-Yehuda, A. Schuster, D. Tsafrir, The resource-as-a-service (RaaS) cloud, in: Proceedings of the 4th USENIX conference on Hot Topics in Cloud Computing, USENIX Association, Boston, MA, June 2012, p. 12.

[47] M. Mao, M. Humphrey, A performance study on the VM startup time in the cloud, in: IEEE 5th International Conference on Cloud Computing (CLOUD), IEEE, June 2012, pp. 423–430.

[48] Halting Problem. http://en.wikipedia.org/wiki/Halting_problem, November 2015.

[49] G. Copil, D. Moldovan, H.L. Truong, S. Dustdar, SYBL: an extensible language for controlling elasticity in cloud applications, in: Proceedings of the 13th IEEE/ACM International Symposium on Cluster, Cloud and Grid Computing (CCGrid), IEEE, Delft, Netherlands, May 2013, pp. 112–119.

[50] T. Lorido-Botran, J. Miguel-Alonso, J.A. Lozano, A review of auto-scaling techniques for elastic applications in cloud environments, J. Grid Comput. 12 (4) (2014) 559–592.

[51] R. Buyya, R. Ranjan, R.N. Calheiros, Intercloud: utility-oriented federation of cloud computing environments for scaling of application services, in: C.H. Hsu, L.T. Yang, J.H. Park, S.S. Yeo (Eds.), Algorithms and Architectures for Parallel Processing, Springer, Berlin, Heidelberg, 2010, pp. 13–31.

[52] P. Pawluk, B. Simmons, M. Smit, M. Litoiu, S. Mankovski, Introducing STRATOS: a cloud broker service, in: IEEE Fifth International Conference on Cloud Computing, IEEE, June 2012, pp. 891–898.

[53] K. Kelly, A cloudbook for the cloud, Luettu 24 (2012) (2007) 30.

[54] The Aeolus Project. http://www.aeolus-project.org, November 2015.

[55] Are Long VM Instance Spin-Up Times in the Cloud Costing You Money? http:// highscalability.com/blog/2011/3/17/are-long-vm-instance-spin-up-times-in-the-cloud-costing-you.html, November 2015.

[56] Why does Azure Deployment Take so Long? http://stackoverflow.com/questions/ 5080445/why-does-azure-deployment-take-so-long, November 2015.

[57] S. Ostermann, A. Iosup, N. Yigitbasi, R. Prodan, T. Fahringer, D. Epema, A performance analysis of EC2 cloud computing services for scientific computing, in: D.R. Avresky, M. Diaz, A. Bode, B. Ciciani, E. Dekel (Eds.), Cloud Computing, Springer, Berlin, Heidelberg, 2010, pp. 115–131.

[58] Z. Hill, J. Li, M. Mao, A. Ruiz-Alvarez, M. Humphrey, Early observations on the performance of Windows Azure, in: Proceedings of the 19th ACM International Symposium on High Performance Distributed Computing, ACM, Chicago, IL, June 2010, pp. 367–376.

[59] Amazon Spot Instances. http://aws.amazon.com/ec2/spot-instances, November 2015.

[60] X. Wu, Z. Shen, R. Wu, Y. Lin, Jump-start cloud: efficient deployment framework for large-scale cloud applications, Concurr. Comput. Pract. Exper. 24 (17) (2012) 2120–2137.

[61] J. Zhu, Z. Jiang, Z. Xiao, Twinkle: a fast resource provisioning mechanism for internet services, in: Proceedings of the IEEE INFOCOM, IEEE, Shanghai, China, April 2011, pp. 802–810.

[62] C. Tang, FVD: a high-performance virtual machine image format for cloud, in: USENIX Annual Technical Conference, June 2011.

[63] C. Peng, M. Kim, Z. Zhang, H. Lei, VDN: virtual machine image distribution network for cloud data centers, in: Proceedings of the IEEE INFOCOM, IEEE, Orlando, FL, March 2012, pp. 181–189.

[64] D. Villegas, N. Bobroff, I. Rodero, J. Delgado, Y. Liu, A. Devarakonda, et al., Cloud federation in a layered service model, J. Comput. Syst. Sci. 78 (5) (2012) 1330–1344.

[65] A. Kivity, D. Laor, G. Costa, P. Enberg, N. Har'El, D. Marti, V. Zolotarov, OSv—optimizing the operating system for virtual machines, in: 2014 USENIX Annual Technical Conference, vol. 1, USENIX Association, June 2014, pp. 61–72.

[66] S. Yi, D. Kondo, A. Andrzejak, Reducing costs of spot instances via checkpointing in the Amazon elastic compute cloud, in: IEEE 3rd International Conference on Cloud Computing (CLOUD), IEEE, July 2010, pp. 236–243.

[67] S. Wee, Debunking real-time pricing in cloud computing, in: Proceedings of the 11th IEEE/ACM International Symposium on Cluster, Cloud and Grid Computing (CCGrid), IEEE, Los Angeles, CA, May 2011, pp. 585–590.

[68] N. Chohan, C. Castillo, M. Spreitzer, M. Steinder, A. Tantawi, C. Krintz, See spot run: using spot instances for mapreduce workflows, in: Proceedings of the 2nd USENIX Conference on Hot Topics in Cloud Computing, USENIX Association, Boston, MA, June 2010, p. 7.

[69] M. Mattess, C. Vecchiola, R. Buyya, Managing peak loads by leasing cloud infrastructure services from a spot market, in: Proceedings of the 12th IEEE International Conference on High Performance Computing and Communications (HPCC), IEEE, Melbourne, Australia, September 2010, pp. 180–188.

[70] A. Andrzejak, D. Kondo, S. Yi, Decision model for cloud computing under SLA constraints, in: IEEE International Symposium on Modeling, Analysis and Simulation of Computer and Telecommunication Systems (MASCOTS), IEEE, 2010, pp. 257–266.

[71] T. Yu, J. Qiu, B. Reinwald, L. Zhi, Q. Wang, N. Wang, Intelligent database placement in cloud environment, in: IEEE 19th International Conference on Web Services (ICWS), IEEE, June 2012, pp. 544–551.

[72] Y.J. Hong, J. Xue, M. Thottethodi, Dynamic server provisioning to minimize cost in an IaaS cloud, in: Proceedings of the ACM SIGMETRICS Joint International Conference on Measurement and Modeling of Computer Systems, ACM, San Jose, CA, June 2011, pp. 147–148.

[73] S. Chaisiri, R. Kaewpuang, B.S. Lee, D. Niyato, Cost minimization for provisioning virtual servers in Amazon elastic compute cloud, in: IEEE 19th International Symposium on Modeling, Analysis and Simulation of Computer and Telecommunication Systems (MASCOTS), IEEE, 2011, pp. 85–95.

[74] J. Sohn, T.G. Robertazzi, S. Luryi, Optimizing computing costs using divisible load analysis, IEEE Trans. Para. Distrib. Syst. 9 (3) (1998) 225–234.

[75] S. Chaisiri, B.S. Lee, D. Niyato, Robust cloud resource provisioning for cloud computing environments, in: IEEE International Conference on Service-Oriented Computing and Applications (SOCA), IEEE, December 2010, pp. 1–8.

[76] S. Chaisiri, B.S. Lee, D. Niyato, Optimal virtual machine placement across multiple cloud providers, in: IEEE Asia-Pacific Services Computing Conference, APSCC, IEEE, December 2009, pp. 103–110.

[77] Z. Gong, X. Gu, J. Wilkes, Press: predictive elastic resource scaling for cloud systems, in: International Conference on Network and Service Management (CNSM), IEEE, October 2010, pp. 9–16.

[78] Z. Shen, S. Subbiah, X. Gu, J. Wilkes, Cloudscale: elastic resource scaling for multi-tenant cloud systems, in: Proceedings of the 2nd ACM Symposium on Cloud Computing, ACM, Cascais, Portugal, October 2011, p. 5.

[79] K. LaCurts, J. Mogul, H. Balakrishnan, Y. Turner, Cicada: introducing predictive guarantees for cloud networks, in: USENIX HotCloud, 2014.

[80] D. Shen, J.L. Hellerstein, Predictive models for proactive network management: application to a production web server, in: IEEE/IFIP Network Operations and Management Symposium, NOMS, IEEE, 2000, pp. 833–846.

[81] A. Chandra, W. Gong, P. Shenoy, Dynamic resource allocation for shared data centers using online measurements, in: K. Jeffay, I. Stoica, K. Wehrle (Eds.), Quality of Service—IWQoS 2003, Springer, Berlin, Heidelberg, 2003, pp. 381–398.

[82] D. Gmach, J. Rolia, L. Cherkasova, A. Kemper, Capacity management and demand prediction for next generation data centers, in: IEEE International Conference on Web Services, ICWS, IEEE, July 2007, pp. 43–50.

[83] N. Vasić, D. Novaković, S. Miučin, D. Kostić, R. Bianchini, Dejavu: accelerating resource allocation in virtualized environments, ACM SIGARCH Computer Architecture News, vol. 40, ACM, New York, NY, 2012, pp. 423–436. No. 1.

[84] S. Dutta, S. Gera, A. Verma, B. Viswanathan, SmartScale: automatic application scaling in enterprise clouds, in: IEEE Fifth International Conference on Cloud Computing, IEEE, 2012, pp. 221–228, http://dx.doi.org/10.1109/CLOUD.2012.12.

[85] W. Fang, Z. Lu, J. Wu, Z. Cao, RPPS: a novel resource prediction and provisioning scheme in cloud data center, in: IEEE Ninth International Conference on Services Computing, IEEE, 2012, pp. 609–616, http://dx.doi.org/10.1109/SCC.2012.47.

[86] J. Huang, C. Li, J. Yu, Resource prediction based on double exponential smoothing in cloud computing, in: Proceedings of 2012 2nd International Conference on Consumer Electronics, Communications and Networks (CECNet), IEEE, Three Gorges, China, 2012, pp. 2056–2060.

[87] S. Islam, J. Keung, K. Lee, A. Liu, Empirical prediction models for adaptive resource provisioning in the cloud, Future Gener. Comput. Syst. 28 (1) (2012) 155–162, http://dx.doi.org/10.1016/j.future.2011.05.027.

[88] R. Prodan, V. Nae, Prediction-based real-time resource provisioning for massively multiplayer online games, Future Gener. Comput. Syst. 25 (7) (2009) 785–793, http://dx.doi.org/10.1016/j.future.2008.11.002.

[89] A.Y. Nikravesh, S.A. Ajila, C.H. Lung, Towards an autonomic auto-scaling prediction system for cloud resource provisioning, in: IEEE/ACM 10th International Symposium on Software Engineering for Adaptive and Self-Managing Systems (SEAMS), IEEE, 2015, pp. 35–45.

[90] P. Bodík, R. Griffith, C. Sutton, A. Fox, M. Jordan, D. Patterson, Statistical machine learning makes automatic control practical for internet datacenters, in: Proceedings of the 2009 Conference on Hot Topics in Cloud Computing, San Diego, CA, June 2009, p. 12.

[91] W. Dawoud, I. Takouna, C. Meinel, Elastic VM for cloud resources provisioning optimization, in: A. Abraham, J.L. Mauri, J.F. Buford, J. Suzuki, S.M. Thampi (Eds.), Advances in Computing and Communications, Springer, Berlin, Heidelberg, 2011, pp. 431–445.

[92] N. Roy, A. Dubey, A. Gokhale, Efficient autoscaling in the cloud using predictive models for workload forecasting, in: IEEE International Conference on Cloud Computing (CLOUD), IEEE, July 2011, pp. 500–507.

[93] S. Parekh, N. Gandhi, J. Hellerstein, D. Tilbury, T. Jayram, J. Bigus, Using control theory to achieve service level objectives in performance management, Real-Time Syst. 23 (1–2) (2002) 127–141.

[94] P. Padala, K.G. Shin, X. Zhu, M. Uysal, Z. Wang, S. Singhal, et al., Adaptive control of virtualized resources in utility computing environments, ACM SIGOPS Operating Systems Review, vol. 41, ACM, Lisboa, Portugal, 2007, pp. 289–302. No. 3.

[95] E. Kalyvianaki, T. Charalambous, S. Hand, Self-adaptive and self-configured CPU resource provisioning for virtualized servers using Kalman filters, in: Proceedings of the 6th International Conference on Autonomic Computing, ACM, Barcelona, Spain, June 2009, pp. 117–126.

[96] P. Padala, K.Y. Hou, K.G. Shin, X. Zhu, M. Uysal, Z. Wang, et al., Automated control of multiple virtualized resources, in: Proceedings of the 4th ACM European Conference on Computer Systems, ACM, Nuremberg, Germany, April 2009, pp. 13–26.

[97] S.M. Park, M. Humphrey, Self-tuning virtual machines for predictable escience, in: Proceedings of the 2009 9th IEEE/ACM International Symposium on Cluster Computing and the Grid, IEEE Computer Society, Shanghai, China, May 2009, pp. 356–363.

[98] L. Wang, J. Xu, M. Zhao, Y. Tu, J.A. Fortes, Fuzzy modeling based resource management for virtualized database systems, in: IEEE 19th International Symposium on Modeling, Analysis and Simulation of Computer and Telecommunication Systems (MASCOTS), IEEE, 2011, pp. 32–42.

[99] A. Ali-Eldin, M. Kihl, J. Tordsson, E. Elmroth, Efficient provisioning of bursty scientific workloads on the cloud using adaptive elasticity control, in: Proceedings of the 3rd Workshop on Scientific Cloud Computing Date, ACM, Delft, Netherlands, June 2012, pp. 31–40.

[100] Z. Chen, Y. Zhu, Y. Di, S. Feng, A dynamic resource scheduling method based on fuzzy control theory in cloud environment, J. Control Sci. Eng. 2015 (2015) 34.

[101] R.N. Calheiros, R. Ranjan, R. Buyya, Virtual machine provisioning based on analytical performance and QoS in cloud computing environments, in: International Conference on Parallel Processing (ICPP), IEEE, Taipei City, Taiwan, September 2011, pp. 295–304.

[102] D. Villela, P. Pradhan, D. Rubenstein, Provisioning servers in the application tier for e-commerce systems, in: Twelfth IEEE International Workshop on Quality of Service, IWQOS, IEEE, Montreal, Québec, Canada, 2004, pp. 57–66.

[103] B. Urgaonkar, G. Pacifici, P. Shenoy, M. Spreitzer, A. Tantawi, An analytical model for multi-tier internet services and its applications, in: E. Smirni (Ed.), ACM SIG-METRICS Performance Evaluation Review, vol. 33, ACM, Banff, Alberta, Canada, 2005, pp. 291–302. No. 1.

[104] B. Urgaonkar, P. Shenoy, A. Chandra, P. Goyal, T. Wood, Agile dynamic provisioning of multi-tier internet applications, ACM Trans. Auton. Adap. Syst. (TAAS) 3 (1) (2008) 1.

[105] Q. Zhang, L. Cherkasova, E. Smirni, A regression-based analytic model for dynamic resource provisioning of multi-tier applications, in: Fourth International Conference on Autonomic Computing, ICAC'07, IEEE, Jacksonville, FL, June 2007, p. 27.

[106] D. Bacigalupo, J. van Hemert, A. Usmani, D.N. Dillenberger, G.B. Wills, S. Jarvis, Resource management of enterprise cloud systems using layered queuing and historical performance models, in: IEEE International Symposium on Parallel and Distributed Processing, Workshops and PhD Forum (IPDPSW), IEEE, Atlanta, GA, 2010, pp. 1–8.

[107] P.D. Kaur, I. Chana, A resource elasticity framework for QoS-aware execution of cloud applications, Future Gener. Comput. Syst. 37 (2014) 14–25.

[108] J. Vilaplana, F. Solsona, I. Teixidó, J. Mateo, F. Abella, J. Rius, A queuing theory model for cloud computing, J. Supercomput. 69 (1) (2014) 492–507.

[109] J. Yin, X. Lu, H. Chen, X. Zhao, N.N. Xiong, System resource utilization analysis and prediction for cloud based applications under bursty workloads, Inform. Sci. 279 (2014) 338–357.

[110] W. Su, J. Hu, C. Lin, S. Shen, SLA-aware tenant placement and dynamic resource provision in SaaS, in: IEEE International Conference on Web Services (ICWS), IEEE, June 2015, pp. 615–622.

[111] J. Li, S. Su, X. Cheng, M. Song, L. Ma, J. Wang, Cost-efficient coordinated scheduling for leasing cloud resources on hybrid workloads, Parallel Comput. 44 (2015) 1–17.

[112] X. Liu, S. Li, W. Tong, A queuing model considering resources sharing for cloud service performance, J. Supercomput. 71 (11) (2015) 4042–4055.

ABOUT THE AUTHORS

Md Abu Naser Bikas is a Ph.D. student at the Department of Computer Science of the University of Illinois at Chicago. His research interests are in the areas of Cloud Computing, Distributed Systems, and Software Engineering. He obtained both his Master's and Bachelor's degree in Computer Science and Engineering from the Shahjalal University of Science & Technology, Bangladesh.

Abdullah Alourani is a Ph.D. student at the Department of Computer Science of the University of Illinois at Chicago. He received his master's degree in Computer Science and Engineering from the DePaul University in Chicago and his bachelor's degree in Computer Science and Engineering from the King Saud University, Saudi Arabia. His current research interests are in the areas of Software Testing, Software Engineering, and Cloud Computing.

Mark Grechanik is an Assistant Professor at the Department of Computer Science of the University of Illinois at Chicago. His research area is software engineering in general, with particular interests in software testing, maintenance, evolution, and reuse. Dr. Grechanik earned his Ph.D. in Computer Science from the Department of Computer Sciences of the University of Texas at Austin. In parallel with his academic activities, he has worked for over 25 years as a software consultant for startups and Fortune 500 companies. Dr. Grechanik is a recipient of best paper awards from competitive conferences, his research is funded by NSF and Microsoft and he holds many patents. His ideas are implemented and used by different companies and organizations. He is a senior member of ACM and a senior member of IEEE and he serves on the ACM SigSoft Executive Committee. Dr. Grechanik is the General Chair in 2016 of the IEEE International Conference on Software Testing, Verification and Validation (ICST'16), the premier conference in all areas related to software quality and he is elected by the popular vote as a member of the Steering Committee of IEEE ICST. Dr. Grechanik also serves on the Editorial board of the Springer Empirical Software Engineering Journal.

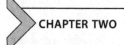

CHAPTER TWO

Input-Sensitive Profiling: A Survey

A. Alourani, M.A.N. Bikas, M. Grechanik
University of Illinois at Chicago, Chicago, IL, United States

Contents

Abstract

Input-sensitive profiling is an automated analysis technique that calculates the resource usages (eg, the memory and the CPU usage) by methods during program execution for different combinations of input values. In addition to enabling developers to estimate the time and space complexities of a program, input-sensitive profiling also allows developers to automatically detect bottlenecks during performance testing, where the performance of a program suddenly worsens for a particular combination of input parameter values. One of the important advantages of this profiling technique is to identify what methods consume more resources (eg, CPU and memory usages) for specific combinations of input values and pinpoint why these methods are responsible for intensive execution time. Hence, developers can understand and optimize performance problems in a program, and they can predict how likely that a program might not scale with increasing the size of the input (eg, adding more users or a larger set of values for a given input parameter). Unfortunately, it is very difficult to identify specific input values from a large number of combinations that lead to performance degradation

Advances in Computers, Volume 103
ISSN 0065-2458
http://dx.doi.org/10.1016/bs.adcom.2016.04.002

31

of programs. The aim of this survey is to explore the input-sensitive profiling problem and discuss its challenges. Some recent contributions of input-sensitive profiling algorithms that were developed to detect performance bottlenecks of a program are investigated and summarized.

1. INTRODUCTION

Over the years, software has become essential to perform many of the tasks of daily life, and thus, it is important to ensure the efficiency and reliability of that software. During software maintenance and evolution, performance profiling is used to guide developers in identifying possible bottlenecks [1], where the performance of a program suddenly worsens for a particular combination of input values.

Traditional profiling has been used since the 1970s [2]. Programs are represented as control flow graphs, where nodes represent methods and edges represent control flows between these methods. Traditional profilers link performance metrics to nodes and paths in control flow graphs or call graphs by gathering performance measurements (eg, execution time) for specific input values [3]. These traditional profilers can help stakeholders to improve the performance of software applications by pinpointing methods that are responsible for excessive resource usage. However, these profiling techniques do not identify how the performances of method executions differ with the increasing size of the input. Running the same method with different combinations of input values often results in different resource consumptions. For instance, a particular method may operate efficiently for a small size of input but proves inadequate when the size of the inputs becomes larger. In addition, the key flaw of traditional profiling techniques is based on the assumption that both the size and the type of the input data are given in advance as a specific combination of values [4]. Thus, the possibility of identifying the performance bottlenecks of a program that depends on the size and the type of the input data is significantly reduced.

Input-sensitive profiling is motivated by the limitations of the traditional profiling techniques to deduce the size and type of the input data for detecting possible degradations during performance testing, where the performance of a program suddenly worsens for a particular combination of input parameter values. The interest of researchers in input-sensitive profiling problems has experienced significant growth in the recent years. We consider a motivating example to illustrate the need for input-sensitive profiling techniques [5]. The COSMOS circuit simulator was originally developed by Randal E. Bryant and his colleagues at Carnegie Mellon University (CMU) [6], and we use it to demonstrate how its method was initially efficient but proved inadequate when the size of the inputs became larger. The circuit simulator was used by a major semiconductor manufacturer company, and the manufacturer modified several methods of the simulator to improve its performance. The approach of hashing on bounded-length name prefixes, which refers to the maximum length of letters defined in mapping signal names to electrical nodes, rather than entire names was used to modify these methods. The simulator speed was increased on all benchmarks due to this modification. However, hierarchical naming schemes were used later when circuits became larger, and many signal names eventually hashed to the same buckets because their names ended up sharing common long prefixes. Consequently, the start-up time of the simulator significantly increased to an unacceptable delay of hours as compared to the range of minutes for a normal start-up time. Analyzing the problem took many days, increased costs, and reduced developer productivity. Many other examples of large software projects that underwent the same kind of problems are reported in the past literature [7].

This chapter is organized as follows: Section 2 presents input-sensitive profiling challenges. Section 3 summarizes and critiques three recent researches on input-sensitive profiling. Section 4 analyzes the related works on input-sensitive profiling and, finally, we conclude in Section 5.

2. INPUT-SENSITIVE PROFILING CHALLENGES

The main problem with profiling is that it is impossible to execute a program with all combinations of all input values, which could be infinite. As a result, engineers try to assess the performance of a program across a representative set of input values. One way to do this is through benchmarking [8], where benchmark inputs represent all input values, and a program that is efficient for the benchmarks is assumed to be efficient for all inputs. However, it is imperative to note that selecting benchmark input values does not guarantee the efficiency of detecting any unknown asymptotic inefficiencies embedded in a program. One of the principal challenges with profiling is the inability to detect performance problems that depend on specific input values and automatically infer the size and the type of the input data whose executions contribute most to possible degradations of a program during performance testing.

Another challenge lies in the profiling of nontrivial applications that involve a large number of combinations of values of input variables. A lot of nontrivial applications contain complex logic embodied in their source code that is expressed by using different nested control flow instructions, where their branch conditions evaluate the expressions according to wide range values of input variables. For instance, 20 inputs of integer type in value range (0–9) yields 10^{20} combinations [4]. In addition to the challenge of efficiency, detecting specific bottlenecks is a challenge. Although some input-sensitive profiling can pinpoint the cause of input variables (eg, the linked list and the array) that are responsible for excessive resource usage, it is difficult to identify the root cause of input variables that encode data in primitive data types (eg, integer type) [9].

 ## 3. RECENT RESEARCHES ON INPUT-SENSITIVE PROFILING

In this survey, we review and summarize three recent contributions of input-sensitive profiling algorithms that are highly representative of main trends in application profiling. These algorithms promise to identify what methods consume more resources (eg, CPU and memory usages) for specific combinations of input values and pinpoint why these methods are responsible for intensive execution time. In the first paper, "Input-Sensitive Profiling," Coppa, Demetrescu, and Finocchi propose an automated profiling methodology that instruments a program with different size of the inputs to assist developers in discovering inefficiencies, where the performance of a program suddenly worsens with the increasing size of the input, and in estimating the time complexity of each method in the program. The important feature of this profiling methodology is the capability to automatically measure the size of the input for a generic source code fragment of a method. In the second paper, "Automating Performance Bottleneck Detection using Search-Based Application Profiling," Shen, Lo, Poshyvanyk, and Grechanik propose an automated methodology to detect bottleneck by utilizing a search-based input-sensitive mechanism. Their main concept is to employ a genetic algorithm to search for a particular combination of input parameter values that improves the objective (eg, execution time) of the fitness function in identifying performance bottlenecks, where the performance of a program suddenly worsens for a particular combination of input values. In the third paper, "Algorithmic Profiling," Zaparanuks and Hauswirth propose an automated profiling methodology for understanding how the resource usage measurements are affected individually by the size of the input, the algorithm (eg, recursions and loops), and the underlying implementation of algorithms (eg, traversing a data structure iteratively or recursively). The important feature of this profiling algorithm is the ability to pinpoint why these methods are responsible for excessive execution time.

3.1 Input-Sensitive Profiling

3.1.1 Summary

Although traditional techniques of performance profiling could help collect important information (eg, execution time) for assessing program behavior and for guiding code optimization to improve implementations that consume intensive resources, they do not identify how a program scales with increasing the size of its input. That is, these techniques do not detect the root causes of scalability problems in software applications. For instance, a method may initially execute efficiently on a particular size of input, but in later releases of the application it may become a bottleneck, where the performance of the application suddenly worsens with the increasing size of the input. In general, traditional profiling techniques lack a suitable way of discovering inefficiencies of methods.

Coppa, Demetrescu, and Finocchi contribute toward the solution called *input-sensitive profiling* by proposing an automated profiling methodology to assist programmers in identifying inefficiencies characterizing the behavior and estimating the time complexity of methods within a program. Aprof, a Valgrind-based tool [10] used to build dynamic profile tools by providing an automatic instrumentation framework to support several operations of memory management, was developed to automatically assess the performance of methods in a program for a specific size of input during performance testing. This profiling technique explores an essential principle in context-sensitive profiling [11], which maps performance metrics to paths in call graphs by automatically linking a cost value (eg, execution time) to a specific size of input instead of to program components in paths (eg, execution traces), including branch conditions, loop statements, or procedure calls.

The authors of Aprof introduced a time-efficient algorithm for computing a metric called *read memory size (RMS)*, which is used to estimate the size of input based on the number of memory cells accessed by a certain method. The main idea of the algorithm is to store the partial RMS data that can be speedily updated during RMS calculation and effortlessly derived when a method is completed. This algorithm reduces the amount of information stored and improves the speed of the algorithm. For a method executed within a program, Aprof automatically collects a set of performance tuples that contain the different values of the RMS linked to the statistically analyzed functions (eg, the maximum and minimum execution time) and generates performance plots that can be analyzed by developers to detect inefficiencies of methods. These plots provide developers with informative visualization insights into how a program behaves in relation to different sizes of its inputs during performance testing.

The effectiveness of Aprof compared to a traditional profiling tool called Gprof [12] was evaluated using a simple word frequency counting program called wf-0.41 [13], which counts the frequency of words using two methods: addword, which is used to add a word to a hash table, and str_tolower, which is used to change all letters of a word to lower case. The ability of both profiling tools to detect the inefficiencies of a method was evaluated using wf-0.41 on two different string lengths of input. In contrast to Gprof, Aprof was able to identify the presence of inefficiencies in the str_tolower method when the size of its input became larger even though this method initially executed efficiently for a small size of input. The cost of the method rises quadratically as the length of the input string increases.

In addition, the efficiency of Aprof was evaluated against two common Valgrind-based tools, memcheck and callgrind, using a set of SPEC CPU2006 benchmarks [14]. Memcheck is used to identify memory-related errors, whereas callgrind is used to produce a branch prediction profiler and generate a cache of a call graph. Although the tools do not solve similar analysis problems, they use the same instrumentation infrastructure as Valgrind, which explains the significant portion of the execution times. In general, the Valgrind tools delivered similar overall execution time despite the facts that callgrind does not trace method read and write memory accesses and memcheck does not trace method call and return, which significantly contribute to a proportion of the execution times. However, when comparing Aprof to memcheck, which likewise utilizes the memory shadowing method, Aprof needs about 20% additional space. To sum up, the input-sensitive profiling technique compared to traditional techniques proves the ability to help developers in detecting inefficiencies and approximating the time complexity of methods within a program. In addition, Aprof delivered an effective and efficient performance profiling solution to detect the inefficiencies of methods in a program.

3.1.2 Critique
Some limitations of input-sensitive profiling technique are discussed that may form a direction for future research. The first limitation is that Aprof

does not estimate the time complexity of the entire program by missing communication between threads and data generated via an operating system (eg, system calls of I/O or network operations). This profiling technique has not been generalized to handle all types of underlying platforms, specifically those that are not eligible to be instrumented by Valgrind [10], which is the underlying implementation of Aprof and is used to build dynamic profile tools by providing an automatic instrumentation framework to support several operations of memory management. In addition, the assumption of computing the time complexity of a method depends on the size of the input and not on the actual values of the input. However, the time complexity of a method is highly associated with the size and the type of its input data. Finally, Aprof often collects a set of performance tuples, which contain the values of the *RMS* linked to the statistically analyzed functions (eg, the maximum and minimum execution time) and generates performance plots upon a single run. Thus, it may fail to detect root causes of scalability problems, specifically those that occur on uncovered bad execution traces by a particular run of a software application.

3.2 Search-Based Profiling

3.2.1 Summary

In the paper, Shen, Luo, Poshyvanyk, and Grechanik address the main problem of profiling nontrivial applications that involve a large number of combinations of input parameter values. A lot of nontrivial applications contain complex logic embodied in the source code, which is expressed by using different nested control flow instructions, where the branch conditions evaluate the expressions according to the wide range values of the input variables. The problem has been inspired by the difficulty of detecting performance problems that depend on specific input values when the performance of the program suddenly worsens for a particular combination of input values during performance testing. Moreover, the problem has been motivated by the possibility to infer the size and the type of the input data whose executions contribute the most to possible bottlenecks automatically. It is also impossible to execute a program with all combinations of all input values, which could be infinite. It is increasingly important to find a way of exploring the input parameter space to enable profilers to automatically extract a specific combination of input values that increase the precision of detecting bottlenecks.

The authors propose a profiling methodology to automate bottleneck discovery by utilizing a search-based input-sensitive mechanism. The main concept of the methodology is to employ a genetic algorithm to search for a particular combination of input parameter values that improve the objective (eg, the execution time) of the fitness function in identifying performance bottlenecks. Genetic algorithm-driven profiler (GA-prof) was developed to automatically and accurately identify performance bottlenecks by integrating an evolutionary search-based heuristic and clustering data mining approach. In addition, the authors make three important contributions in the paper. First, GA-prof is the first profiling technique that automatically explores the input parameter space to identify performance degradations. Second, GA-prof is an efficient profiler for assessing a large number of potential combinations of inputs and identifying bottlenecks accurately. Finally, GA-prof and its experimental results are made available to the public.

The authors of GA-prof introduced an efficient profiling algorithm for exploring a large number of potential combinations of inputs to detect performance degradations accurately. An evolutionary algorithm (genetic algorithm) is used for exploring the different permutations of inputs. A key element of genetic algorithms is a fitness function that is used to guide the entire search methodology by mapping the inputs to the elapsed execution times. The set of input values that maximizes the fitness function and leads to potential bottlenecks is chosen by applying the genetic operators (eg, the selector, crossover, and mutation) for further investigation of performance bottlenecks. These sets are categorized into good input sets that likely steer the application toward computationally expensive paths and longer execution times. Conversely, the bad input sets lead to comparatively lower expensive paths and execution times. A list of methods ranked in descending order, where a higher ranking signifies a high chance of causing bottlenecks, is computed using the different trace statistics with the traces grouped into good and bad execution traces. The good traces consume more resources (eg, the memory) and cause longer execution times, whereas the bad traces are neither resource nor time intensive. Eventually, developers can identify possible performance bottlenecks from the top of that list for further code optimizations to improve implementations.

The authors evaluated the performance of GA-prof on three web-based applications: Agilefant [15], an enterprise-level project management system; DellDVDStore [16], an online DVD renting site; and JPetStore [17], a Java implementation of PetStore. These web-based applications are open source, rely on databases, and communicate with back-end functions that use web URLs as data inputs. To evaluate the effectiveness of GA-prof in identifying a specific combination of input values whose executions contribute most to possible degradations, GA-prof performs multiple transactions concurrently, collects the parallel executed traces, and computes the respective execution times of these applications. The experimental results show that GA-prof could effectively find the possible combinations of URLs that consume more resources (eg, the memory) and cause computationally intensive execution times. Furthermore, the effectiveness of GA-prof in detecting performance problems that depend on specific input values was evaluated by randomly injecting artificial bottlenecks into these applications. The experimental results show that GA-prof has a higher probability of identifying the bottlenecks in all three web-based applications. It has an 80% probability of identifying at least five bottlenecks. However, there were times when certain bottlenecks ranked low on the list but reappeared at the top of the list. The authors note that the occurrence is anticipated because they are using a search-based approach that can select some values that lack optimization.

In addition, the performance effectiveness of GA-prof compared to the closest competitive approach called FOREPOST [18], which uses a machine learning approach to create models that associate input classes according to application performance and produces a list of methods ranked in descending order on the basis of their performance bottlenecks, was evaluated using two of the applications: JPetStore and DellDVDStore. The experimental results demonstrated that GA-prof identified more bottlenecks than FOREPOST even though both techniques can identify the correct input sets, which steer the execution of the application along more computationally intensive paths. In general, GA-prof is equally effective in detecting bottlenecks as FOREPOST. To sum up, the proposed profiling technique proves the ability to help developers in exploring a large number of potential combinations of inputs to identify performance degradations. Moreover, GA-prof delivered an effective and accurate performance profiling solution to detect bottlenecks in the program.

3.2.2 Critique

In the paper, the authors have pointed a few limitations with the methodology of GA-prof. A genetic algorithm may generate invalid URLs that could adversely affect the results. Thus, GA-prof may require additional functions that ensure that only valid URLs are generated. GA-prof does not identify the methods that may utilize intensive resources without substantially affecting performance. The injection of artificial bottlenecks may not cover some bottlenecks that due to external sources (eg, the delay in network communications), and hot spots may not always appear in random areas of the program. Finally, although GA-prof has a few limitations, it enables developers to understand and optimize performance problems in a program by efficiently exploring a large number of potential combinations of input values to precisely detect performance bottlenecks.

3.3 Algorithmic Profiling

3.3.1 Summary

Traditional profilers link performance metrics to nodes and paths in control flow graphs (or *call graphs*) by gathering performance measurements (eg, execution time) for specific input values to help developers improve the performance of software applications by identifying what methods consume more resources (eg, CPU and memory usage). However, these profiling techniques do not pinpoint why these methods are responsible for intensive resource usages and do not identify how the resource consumptions of the same method differ with the increasing size of the input (eg, the number of nodes in an input linked list or a tree or a bigger input array). That is, when executing an application with different sizes of inputs, the same method of this application often consumes different resources. A main problem with profiling techniques is that they do not explain how the cost that measures resource usage is affected individually by the size of the input, the algorithm (eg, recursions and loops), and the underlying implementation of algorithms (eg, traversing a data structure iteratively or recursively). Traditional profilers calculate resource usage by combining these factors and provide limited information by reporting the overall cost. It is increasingly important to find a way of identifying how individual factors, including the size of input, algorithm, and implementation, impact the cost to uncover the relationship of the execution cost to the program input.

Zaparanuks and Hauswirth propose an automated profiling methodology to help developers to detect algorithmic (eg, recursions and loops) inefficiencies by inferring a cost function of a program that relates the cost to the input size and to predict how the resource usage would scale with increasing the size of the input. AlgoProf was developed to automatically identify algorithms (eg, recursions and loops) in a program and infer the time complexity of each algorithm for a specific algorithmic step (eg, the total number of loop iterations) during performance testing. An important feature of this profiling technique is the ability to pinpoint why methods are responsible for intensive resource usages (eg, the CPU and memory) and execution times. Aside from detecting the root causes of scalability problems in a program, this technique can address the problem of measuring the size of the input automatically.

The authors introduced an algorithmic profiler for computing the cost function of a program by identifying algorithms (eg, loops and recursions) and their inputs to measure their sizes (eg, the number of nodes in a linked list), costs (eg, the execution times of loop iterations), and generated performance plots that mapped input size to the cost, ie, they compute cost functions for individual algorithms (eg, loops and recursions). This technique allows developers to make an accurate estimate of the computational cost as a function of algorithms (eg, loops and recursions) based on multiple program runs. The profiling technique employs cost metrics based on a repetition data structure access, such as the execution times of loop iterations, as compared with the execution times of the whole method that is used by traditional profiling techniques. These traditional techniques provide a single cost value, such as hotness (eg, longer execution times), whereas the algorithmic profiler provides much deeper insight into a function that maps the cost to the size and type of the input. Thus, the algorithmic complexity can be inferred more accurately by using cost functions to detect algorithmic inefficiencies. The algorithmic profiler enables developers to understand how the resource usage measurements are affected by the size of the input, the algorithm, and the type of underlying implementation individually. Aside from identifying the root causes of scalability problems in a program, this technique pinpoints why methods are responsible for intensive resource usages (eg, the CPU and memory) and execution times.

The effectiveness of AlgoProf in detecting algorithmic (eg, recursions and loops) inefficiencies was evaluated with a number of programs that implement different algorithms (eg, recursions and loops). Every program uses one data structure type, eg, an array, a linked list, a tree, or a graph. AlgoProf was able to estimate the algorithmic complexities of all data structures in the programs accurately, along with inferring their cost functions to detect algorithmic inefficiencies. Furthermore, the ability of AlgoProf to identify the root causes of scalability problems was evaluated using a Java program that requires the assignment of a larger array when the size of array runs out of space. AlgoProf shows a plot that links a cost (eg, execution times) with the growing array. If the array is grown by a single element at a time, the cost becomes quadratic or worse, ie, exponential. If the array is grown by doubling the size and changing a single line of the source code, the cost can be reduced to a linear function. To sum up, the proposed profiling technique proves to have the ability to help developers detect algorithmic inefficiencies and pinpoint why methods are responsible for intensive resource usage (eg, the CPU and memory) and execution time. Moreover, AlgoProf provided an effective performance profiling solution to estimate the time complexity and detect algorithmic inefficiencies of a method in a program.

3.3.2 Critique

Although AlgoProf overcomes a number of problems associated with traditional profiling, it has several limitations that require further research. The first limitation is that AlgoProf computes only approximate instead of exact cost functions of algorithms (eg, recursions and loops) within a program. AlgoProf can infer a cost function for only algorithms (eg, recursions and loops) that operate on recursive data structures because it is difficult to determine the size of the inputs for algorithms (eg, mathematical functions) that operate on primitive data types (eg, integer). Although AlgoProf can handle multiple threads by creating a profile for every individual thread, it does not evaluate communication between threads. Furthermore, the main limitation of AlgoProf is the time and space overhead. AlgoProf consumes a large amount of data storage and resource when taking complete snapshots of the repetition data structure (eg, lists, trees, and graphs) at every access and storing the complete snapshots in memory, which is wasteful. AlgoProf may cluster repetition data structures (eg, lists, trees, and graphs) into algorithms (eg, loops and recursions) and a notion of input that differs from a developer's instincts on how the application should operate. Finally, the assumption of using an algorithm (eg, loops and recursions) by including the input and ways of measuring and proposing cost is questionable because it was based on a developer's intuition.

3.4 Synthesis

This survey demonstrates that these three studies advanced the theory and practice of input-sensitive profiling as they proposed profiling techniques that enabled developers to detect performance bottlenecks automatically, where the performance of a program suddenly worsens for a particular size and type of input. A limitation of the traditional techniques is the absence of research into how the size and type of input affects/impacts these performance bottlenecks. These studies made contributions that addressed the limitations of the traditional profiling techniques for detecting performance bottlenecks by taking into account specific sizes and types of input. In our future work, we will explore a combination of these algorithms to produce more effective and efficient performance profiling solutions for further code optimizations.

Coppa *et al.* and Zaparanuks *et al.* address the root causes of scalability problems by identifying how a program scales when the size of its input increases, whereas Shen *et al.* address the problem of exploring the input parameter space to extract a specific combination of input values that can help detect bottlenecks more precisely. Alternatively, Shen *et al.* propose an automated profiling methodology to explore efficiently a large number of potential combinations of input values to precisely detect performance degradations. In contrast, Coppa *et al.*'s automated profiling methodology assists programmers in identifying performance bottlenecks and estimates the time complexity of the methods within a profiled program. On the other hand, Zaparanuks *et al.* propose an automated profiling methodology for understanding how the resource usage measurements are affected individually by the size of the input, the algorithm (eg, recursions and loops), and the underlying implementation of algorithms (eg, traversing a data structure iteratively or recursively). Aside from measuring the size of the input in a program automatically, this technique pinpoints methods that are responsible for intensive resource usages (eg, the CPU and memory) and execution times.

Coppa *et al.* introduced an algorithm suitable for computing a metric known as the *RMS*, which is used in the estimation of the input size based on the number of memory cells that have been accessed by a method. In contrast, Zaparanuks *et al.* introduced an algorithmic profiler suitable for computing the cost function of a program that links a program input to cost metrics, which is used in the estimation of the size of input (eg, the number of nodes in a linked list or a tree or the size of an array) by traversing a data structure (eg, lists, trees, and graphs) iteratively or recursively. Zaparanuks *et al.* used cost metrics based on a data structure analysis, whereas Coppa *et al.* used cost metrics based on a low-level memory accesses to estimate the time complexity of a method. The algorithm introduced by Zaparanuks *et al.*, unlike the one introduced by Coppa *et al.*, is capable of providing insights into the root causes of performance bottlenecks by focusing on source code statements (eg, loop statements) and avoiding utilizing physical memory reads and writes as the units of cost assessment. In contrast, the algorithm introduced by Coppa *et al.* is more efficient in estimating the time complexity of a method by tracing low-level memory accesses than the one introduced by Zaparanuks *et al.* On the other hand, Shen *et al.* introduced a profiling algorithm suitable for exploring a large number of potential input combinations and identifying bottlenecks by integrating an evolutionary search-based heuristic and clustering data mining mechanism. Shen *et al.* employs a search-based approach, whereas Coppa *et al.* and Zaparanuks *et al.* employ empirical models. Although these algorithms employ different approaches, they produce accurate and efficient profiling results for assessing program behavior and for guiding code optimization.

The effectiveness of Aprof developed by Coppa *et al.* compared to a traditional profiling tool called Gprof [12] was evaluated using a simple word frequency counting program. In contrast to Gprof, Aprof was able to identify the presence of inefficiencies in a method when the size of its input became larger. The efficiency of Aprof developed by Coppa *et al.* was analyzed by delivering less overall execution time and an additional 20% space compared to competitive traditional profiling tools. The effectiveness of the GA-prof tool developed by Shen *et al.* was analyzed by finding input combinations that cause performance bottlenecks. The performance effectiveness of GA-prof developed by Shen *et al.* compared to the closest competitive approach called FOREPOST was evaluated using nontrivial web applications. The experimental results demonstrated that GA-prof is equally effective in detecting bottlenecks as FOREPOST. Finally, the effectiveness of AlgoProf developed by Zaparanuks in detecting algorithmic (eg, recursions and loops) inefficiencies was evaluated with a number of programs. AlgoProf was able to estimate the algorithmic complexities of all data structures in the programs accurately, along with inferring their cost functions to detect algorithmic inefficiencies. Although these tools apply different techniques, they enable developers to detect performance bottlenecks for further code optimizations. To sum up, the synthesis has discussed the findings, similarities, and differences obtained by these studies that focused on input-sensitive profiling techniques. These studies have proposed solutions to the problems associated with traditional algorithm profilers. Although these profiling techniques have some limitations, they can effectively and accurately detect performance bottlenecks.

4. RELATED WORK

The interest of researchers in input-sensitive profiling problems has experienced significant growth in recent years. We provide a brief survey on related work of input-sensitive profiling algorithms that are highly representative of main trends in program profiling.

4.1 Scalability Problems

Several techniques for input-sensitive profiling have been studied in Refs. [19–23] to address scalability problems. Toffola et al. [19] employed a memoization-based mechanism by a scalable comparing of inputs and outputs instead of objects of all method calls to find identical methods that frequently execute similar computations. Coppa et al. [20] introduced an extended algorithm of the work [7] that was suitable for computing a developed metric of the RMS, which is used in the estimation of the input size performed by nondeterministic memory accesses by the operating system kernel as auxiliary threads (eg, system calls of I/O or network operations). Marin et al. [21] described how the performance of an application scale for different sizes of its inputs; utilizing multiple-run data depends on specific input parameters. Xiao et al. [22] proposed a multiexecution profiling technique to detect unscalable methods with increasing the size of its input. Goldsmith et al. [23] introduced a technique to predict how an application's performance scales given different sizes of workloads for each routine in a program by linking the execution time to the input size. This technique also enables software engineers to detect the bugs in an application's performance that are caused by asymptotic inefficiencies to decrease the computation complexity of a program. On the other hands, some works [24–26] proposed techniques based on different execution and code patterns that might lead to performance problems. They do not identify how a program scales with increasing the size of its input.

4.2 Program Performance Prediction

Several studies have focused on program performance prediction by taking into account different input-sensitive techniques. Chattopadhyay used a search-based approach by exploring the input domain using different path programs to estimate the time complexity of the entire program [27]. Nistor et al. used a pattern recognition approach using a common input in smartphone applications by providing insights into how the patterns might grow when the size of its input became larger [28]. Puschner et al. [29] proposed a technique based on an evolutionary algorithm to identify the paths of a program for a specific input domain during performance testing. This technique explores the entire program locality depending on a couple of training runs of the program. Qi et al. [30] introduced a technique by combining multiple paths to enable path-based testing. A couple paths are combined as long as they have a similar input–output relationship (eg, the same expression of output). Kwon *et al.* [31] proposed a technique based on a machine learning algorithm utilizing multiple training inputs to predict the performance of a smartphone application. However, the technique was measured on the intensity of the CPU with a few user interactions. Hazelwood *et al.* [32] analyzed the performance problems related to predicated code and whenever the input of a program changes utilizing dynamic profiling to detect hard-to-predict branches for a given input set.

4.3 Code Optimization

Other techniques have focused on code optimization utilizing various input-sensitive approaches. Coppa [33] employed a visualization-based approach by providing interactive graphical charts of performance profiles to pinpoint the most crucial methods in a program and estimate their time complexities. Ding *et al.* [34] proposed a self-refining input-sensitive algorithmic autotuning approach that determines what algorithmic optimization to use based on the varying input combinations. The authors used clustering to find automatically similar input sets in the multidimensional feature space and then used a statistical learning model to build an input classifier to make input-sensitive algorithmic choice by optimizing the search space and input space complexity. Küstner *et al.* [35] proposed an argument controlled profiling, which focused on the changing value of functions arguments as part of the profiling context in order to guide code optimization. This approach is useful in finding performance problems in recursive functions. Likewise, several studies [36–40] addressed the problem of input-centric dynamic program optimizations, where inputs of the program have to be characterized differently depending on the target application behavior. These studies respond to dynamic changes in the behavior of the system, unlike Ref. [34], which adapt its configurations proactively depending on the inputs of the program.

4.4 Task Scheduling Optimization

Kofler *et al.* [41] proposed an input-sensitive approach to automatically distribute OpenCL workloads over multiple heterogeneous devices that consist multicore CPUs and GPUs. They performed the workload prediction based on an Artificial Neural Networks by analyzing static program features (eg, floating-point operations, the number of loops, etc.) and dynamic program features (eg, data transfer size and runtime overhead, etc.) with varying input data. Similarly, Grasso *et al.*, Wen *et al.*, and Grewe *et al.* [42–44] proposed machine learning-based OpenCL task scheduling schemes to partition kernels between multiple devices automatically by considering input data size at runtime. Runtime profiling used in Ref. [41] to generate the distribution model that may introduce significant runtime overhead, whereas Grasso et al., Wen et al., and Grewe et al. [42–44] used offline training data to build their predictor, where the prediction accuracy depends on the size of training data set. Some other studies [36,45,46] also explored the effect of different input sizes to perform some task scheduling optimizations on GPU program.

4.5 Test Generation Analysis

There are a few literatures on test generation analyses to address performance problems. Burnim et al. [47] proposed a technique that creates tests based on the input of a program to identify the worst-case complexity. Pradel et al. [48] proposed a technique that generates tests for a concurrent program to perform performance regression testing automatically. Killian et al. [49] focused on the automatic identification of performance bugs in distributed systems by generating random simulations tests. However, this technique does not estimate the time complexity of the entire program. Wall et al. [50] introduced the initial metrics for measuring the representative data for various input sets. The work defined the similarities and differences within referenced global variables, procedure calls, and basic blocks.

4.6 Data-Dependence Profiling

Some works targeted data dependence profiling have been studied in literature. Zhang et al. [51] designed a data dependence distance profiling tool called Alchemist to identify the existence of concurrency in programs automatically. The tool identifies constructs in program regions to be selected for asynchronous execution. Wu et al. [52] used profiling technique based on data dependences to guide the selection process of compiler-driven task targeted at thread level speculation. Chen et al. [53] designed a data dependence profiling technique aimed at speculative optimizations.

5. CONCLUSION

In this survey, we review and summarize three recent studies of input-sensitive profiling algorithms that identify methods that consume more resources (eg, CPU and memory usages) for specific types and sizes of input and give causes why these methods are responsible for excessive execution time. These studies have proposed solutions to the problems associated with traditional algorithm profilers. In the first paper, "Input-Sensitive Profiling," Coppa, Demetrescu, and Finocchi propose an automated profiling methodology to assist programmers in identifying inefficiencies characterizing the behavior and estimating the time complexity of methods within a profiled program. In the second paper, "Automating Performance Bottleneck Detection using Search-Based Application Profiling," Shen, Lo, Poshyvanyk, and Grechanik propose an automated profiling methodology to efficiently explore a large number of potential combinations of input values to detect performance degradations precisely. In the third paper, "Algorithmic Profiling," Zaparanuks and Hauswirth propose profiling methodology to assist programmers in understanding how the cost that measures resource usage is affected by the size of the input, the algorithm, and the underlying implementation individually. Finally, although these profiling techniques have some limitations, these accurate and efficient profiling techniques enable developers to understand and optimize performance problems in a profiled program.

REFERENCES

[1] N. Chapin, J.E. Hale, K.M. Khan, J.F. Ramil, W.G. Tan, Types of software evolution and software maintenance, J. Softw. Maint. Evol. Res. Pract. 13 (1) (2001) 3–30.
[2] D.E. Knuth, F.R. Stevenson, Optimal measurement points for program frequency counts, BIT Numer. Math. 13 (3) (1973) 313–322.
[3] J.M. Spivey, Fast, accurate call graph profiling, Softw. Pract. Exp. 34 (3) (2004) 249–264.
[4] D. Shen, Q. Luo, D. Poshyvanyk, M. Grechanik, Automating performance bottleneck detection using search-based application profiling, in: Proceedings of the 2015 International Symposium on Software Testing and Analysis, ACM, Baltimore, MD, July 2015, pp. 270–281.
[5] R.E. Bryant. Personal communication, September 2011.
[6] D. Beatty, K. Brace, R.E. Bryant, K. Cho, L. Huang, User's Guide to COSMOS, a Compiled Simulator for MOS Circuits, Computer Science Department, Carnegie Melon University, Miami, FL, 1987.
[7] E. Coppa, C. Demetrescu, I. Finocchi, Input-sensitive profiling, ACM SIGPLAN Not. 47 (6) (2012) 89–98.
[8] W. Pfeiffer, N.J. Wright, Modeling and predicting application performance on parallel computers using HPC challenge benchmarks, in: IEEE International Symposium on Parallel and Distributed Processing. IPDPS, IEEE, Miami, FL, April 2008, pp. 1–12.
[9] D. Zaparanuks, M. Hauswirth, Algorithmic profiling, ACM SIGPLAN Not. 47 (6) (2012) 67–76.
[10] N. Nethercote, J. Seward, Valgrind: a framework for heavyweight dynamic binary instrumentation, ACM SIGPLAN Not. 42 (6) (2007) 89–100.

[11] G. Ammons, T. Ball, J.R. Larus, Exploiting hardware performance counters with flow and context sensitive profiling, ACM SIGPLAN Not. 32 (5) (1997) 85–96.

[12] S.L. Graham, P.B. Kessler, M.K. Mckusick, Gprof: a call graph execution profiler, ACM SIGPLAN Not. 17 (6) (1982) 120–126.

[13] Project. wf: simple word frequency counter (Build Date: Jan 15 2012). http://www.rpm-find.net//linux/RPM/archive.fedoraproject.org/fedora/linux/releases/17/Everything/source/SRPMS/w/wf-0.41-6.fc17.src.html, 2015.

[14] J.L. Henning, SPEC CPU2006 benchmark descriptions, ACM SIGARCH Comput. Archit. News 34 (4) (2006) 1–17.

[15] Agilefant, http://www.agilefant.com, December 2015.

[16] DellDVDStore, http://linux.dell.com/dvdstore, December 2015.

[17] JPetStore, https://github.com/mybatis/jpetstore-6, December 2015.

[18] M. Grechanik, C. Fu, Q. Xie, Automatically finding performance problems with feedback-directed learning software testing, in: 34th International Conference on Software Engineering (ICSE), IEEE, Zurich, Switzerland, June 2012, pp. 156–166.

[19] L. Della Toffola, M. Pradel, T.R. Gross, Performance problems you can fix: a dynamic analysis of memoization opportunities, in: OOPSLA 2015 Proceedings of the 2015 ACM SIGPLAN International Conference on Object-Oriented Programming, Systems, Languages, and Applications, ACM, Pittsburgh, PA, October 2015, pp. 607–622.

[20] E. Coppa, C. Demetrescu, I. Finocchi, R. Marotta, Multithreaded input-sensitive profiling, arXiv Preprint (2013). arXiv:1304.3804.

[21] G. Marin, J. Mellor-Crummey, Cross-architecture performance predictions for scientific applications using parameterized models, ACM SIGMETRICS Perform. Eval. Rev. 32 (1) (2004) 2–13.

[22] X. Xiao, S. Han, D. Zhang, T. Xie, Context-sensitive delta inference for identifying workload-dependent performance bottlenecks, in: Proceedings of the 2013 International Symposium on Software Testing and Analysis, ACM, Lugano, Switzerland, July 2013, pp. 90–100.

[23] S.F. Goldsmith, A.S. Aiken, D.S. Wilkerson, Measuring empirical computational complexity, in: Proceedings of the 6th Joint Meeting of the European Software Engineering Conference and the ACM SIGSOFT Symposium on the Foundations of Software Engineering, ACM, Dubrovnik, Croatia, September 2007, pp. 395–404.

[24] G. Jin, L. Song, X. Shi, J. Scherpelz, S. Lu, Understanding and detecting real-world performance bugs, ACM SIGPLAN Not. 47 (6) (2012) 77–88.

[25] K. Nguyen, G. Xu, Cachetor: detecting cacheable data to remove bloat, in: Proceedings of the 2013 9th Joint Meeting on Foundations of Software Engineering, ACM, Saint Petersburg, Russia, August 2013, pp. 268–278.

[26] A. Nistor, L. Song, D. Marinov, S. Lu, Toddler: detecting performance problems via similar memory-access patterns, in: Proceedings of the 2013 International Conference on Software Engineering, IEEE Press, San Francisco, CA, May 2013, pp. 562–571.

[27] S. Chattopadhyay, L.K. Chong, A. Roychoudhury, Program performance spectrum, ACM SIGPLAN Not. 48 (5) (2013) 65–76.

[28] A. Nistor, L. Ravindranath, SunCat: helping developers understand and predict performance problems in Smartphone applications, in: Proceedings of the 2014 International Symposium on Software Testing and Analysis, ACM, San Jose, CA, July 2014, pp. 282–292.

[29] P. Puschner, R. Nossal, Testing the results of static worst-case execution-time analysis, in: Proceedings of the 19th IEEE Real-Time Systems Symposium, IEEE, Madrid, Spain, December 1998, pp. 134–143.

[30] D. Qi, H.D. Nguyen, A. Roychoudhury, Path exploration based on symbolic output, ACM Trans. Softw. Eng. Methodol. 22 (4) (2013) 32.

[31] Y. Kwon, S. Lee, H. Yi, D. Kwon, S. Yang, B.G. Chun, L. Huang, P. Maniatis, M. Naik, Y. Paek, Mantis: automatic performance prediction for smartphone applications, in: Proceedings of the 2013 USENIX Conference on Annual Technical Conference, USENIX Association, San Jose, CA, June 2013, pp. 297–308.

[32] K.M. Hazelwood, T.M. Conte, A lightweight algorithm for dynamic if-conversion during dynamic optimization, in: Proceedings of the International Conference on Parallel Architectures and Compilation Techniques, IEEE, Philadelphia, PA, 2000, pp. 71–80.

[33] E. Coppa, An interactive visualization framework for performance analysis, in: Proceedings of the 8th International Conference on Performance Evaluation Methodologies and Tools, December, ICST (Institute for Computer Sciences, Social-Informatics and Telecommunications Engineering), Bratislava, Slovakia, 2014, pp. 159–164.

[34] Y. Ding, J. Ansel, K. Veeramachaneni, X. Shen, U.M. O'Reilly, S. Amarasinghe, Autotuning algorithmic choice for input sensitivity, in: PLDI, 2014, pp. 379–390.

[35] T. Küstner, J. Weidendorfer, T. Weinzierl, Argument controlled profiling, in: Euro-Par 2009—Parallel Processing Workshops, Springer, Berlin and Heidelberg, 2010, pp. 177–184.

[36] M. Samadi, A. Hormati, M. Mehrara, J. Lee, S. Mahlke, Adaptive input-aware compilation for graphics engines, ACM SIGPLAN Not. 47 (6) (2012, June) 13–22.

[37] K. Tian, Y. Jiang, E.Z. Zhang, X. Shen, An input-centric paradigm for program dynamic optimizations, ACM SIGPLAN Not. 45 (10) (2010) 125–139.

[38] G. Karsai, A. Ledeczi, J. Sztipanovits, G. Peceli, G. Simon, T. Kovacshazy, An approach to self-adaptive software based on supervisory control, in: Self-Adaptive Software: Applications, Springer, Berlin and Heidelberg, 2003, pp. 24–38.

[39] X. Li, M.J. Garzarán, D. Padua, A dynamically tuned sorting library, in: International Symposium on Code Generation and Optimization. CGO 2004, IEEE, Palo Alto, CA, March 2004, pp. 111–122.

[40] N. Thomas, G. Tanase, O. Tkachyshyn, J. Perdue, N.M. Amato, L. Rauchwerger, A framework for adaptive algorithm selection in STAPL, in: Proceedings of the Tenth ACM SIGPLAN Symposium on Principles and Practice of Parallel Programming, ACM, Chicago, IL, June 2005, pp. 277–288.

[41] K. Kofler, I. Grasso, B. Cosenza, T. Fahringer, An automatic input-sensitive approach for heterogeneous task partitioning, in: Proceedings of the 27th International ACM Conference on International Conference on Supercomputing, ACM, Eugene, OR, June 2013, pp. 149–160.

[42] I. Grasso, K. Kofler, B. Cosenza, T. Fahringer, Automatic problem size sensitive task partitioning on heterogeneous parallel systems, ACM SIGPLAN Not. 48 (8) (2013) 281–282.

[43] Y. Wen, Z. Wang, M. O'Boyle, Smart multi-task scheduling for OpenCL programs on CPU/GPU heterogeneous platforms, in: Proceedings of the 21st Annual IEEE International Conference on High Performance Computing (HiPC'14), 2014.

[44] D. Grewe, Z. Wang, M.F. O'Boyle, OpenCL task partitioning in the presence of GPU contention, in: Languages and Compilers for Parallel Computing, Springer International Publishing, San Jose, CA, September 2013, pp. 87–101.

[45] Y. Liu, E.Z. Zhang, X. Shen, A cross-input adaptive framework for GPU program optimizations, in: IEEE International Symposium on Parallel & Distributed Processing. IPDPS 2009, IEEE, Rome, Italy, May 2009, pp. 1–10.

[46] A. Magni, D. Grewe, N. Johnson, Input-aware auto-tuning for directive-based GPU programming, in: Proceedings of the 6th Workshop on General Purpose Processor Using Graphics Processing Units, ACM, Houston, TX, March 2013, pp. 66–75.

[47] J. Burnim, S. Juvekar, K. Sen, WISE: Automated test generation for worst-case complexity, in: IEEE 31st International Conference on Software Engineering. ICSE 2009, IEEE, Vancouver, British Columbia, Canada, May 2009, pp. 463–473.

[48] M. Pradel, M. Huggler, T.R. Gross, Performance regression testing of concurrent classes, in: Proceedings of the 2014 International Symposium on Software Testing and Analysis, ACM, San Jose, CA, July 2014, pp. 13–25.

[49] C. Killian, K. Nagaraj, S. Pervez, R. Braud, J.W. Anderson, R. Jhala, Finding latent performance bugs in systems implementations, in: Proceedings of the Eighteenth ACM SIGSOFT International Symposium on Foundations of Software Engineering, ACM, Santa Fe, NM, November 2010, pp. 17–26.

[50] D.W. Wall, Predicting program behavior using real or estimated profiles, in: Proceedings of the SIGPLAN '91 Conference on Programming Language Design and Implementation, ACM SIGPLAN Notices 26 (6), Toronto, Canada, June 1991, pp. 59–70.

[51] X. Zhang, A. Navabi, S. Jagannathan, Alchemist: a transparent dependence distance profiling infrastructure, in: Proceedings of the 7th Annual IEEE/ACM International Symposium on Code Generation and Optimization, IEEE Computer Society, Seattle, WA, March 2009, pp. 47–58.

[52] P. Wu, A. Kejariwal, C. Caşcaval, Compiler-driven dependence profiling to guide program parallelization, in: Languages and Compilers for Parallel Computing, Springer, Berlin and Heidelberg, 2008, pp. 232–248.

[53] T. Chen, J. Lin, X. Dai, W.C. Hsu, P.C. Yew, Data dependence profiling for speculative optimizations, in: Compiler Construction, Springer, Berlin and Heidelberg, 2004, pp. 57–72.

ABOUT THE AUTHORS

Abdullah Alourani is a Ph.D. student at the Department of Computer Science of the University of Illinois at Chicago. He received his master's degree in Computer Science and Engineering from the DePaul University in Chicago and his bachelor's degree in Computer Science and Engineering from the King Saud University, Saudi Arabia. His current research interests are in the areas of Software Testing, Software Engineering, and Cloud Computing.

Md Abu Naser Bikas is a Ph.D. student at the department of computer science of the University of Illinois at Chicago. His research interests are in the areas of Cloud Computing, Distributed Systems, and Software Engineering. He obtained both his Master's and Bachelor's degree in Computer Science and Engineering from the Shahjalal University of Science & Technology, Bangladesh.

Mark Grechanik is an Assistant Professor at the Department of Computer Science of the University of Illinois at Chicago. His research area is software engineering in general, with particular interests in software testing, maintenance, evolution, and reuse. Dr. Grechanik earned his Ph.D. in Computer Science from the Department of Computer Sciences of the University of Texas at Austin. In parallel with his academic activities, he has worked for over 25 years as a software consultant for startups and Fortune 500 companies. Dr. Grechanik is a recipient of best paper awards from competitive conferences, his research is funded by NSF and Microsoft and he holds many patents. His ideas are implemented and used by different companies and organizations. He is a senior member of ACM and a senior member of IEEE and he serves on the ACM SigSoft Executive Committee. Dr. Grechanik is the General Chair in 2016 of the IEEE International Conference on Software Testing, Verification and Validation (ICST'16), the premier conference in all areas related to software quality and he is elected by the popular vote as a member of the Steering Committee of IEEE ICST. Dr. Grechanik also serves on the Editorial board of the Springer Empirical Software Engineering Journal.

CHAPTER THREE

Recent Advances in Regression Testing Techniques

H. Do*
*University of North Texas, Denton, TX, USA

Contents

Abstract

Software systems and their environment change are continuous. They are enhanced, corrected, and ported to new platforms. These changes can affect a system adversely, thus software engineers perform regression testing to ensure the quality of the modified systems. Regression testing is an integral part of most major software projects, but as projects grow larger and the number of tests increases, performing regression testing becomes more costly. To address this problem, many researchers and practitioners have proposed and empirically evaluated various regression testing techniques, such as regression test selection, test case prioritization, and test suite minimization. Recent surveys on these techniques indicate that this research area continues to grow, heuristics and the types of data utilized become diverse, and wider application domains have been considered. This chapter presents the current status and the trends of three regression testing techniques and discusses recent advances of each technique.

1. INTRODUCTION

Regression testing is one of the most common means for ensuring the quality of software products during development cycles and it is almost universally employed by software organizations [1]. It is important for ensuring software quality, but it is also expensive, accounting for a large proportion of software production costs. For example, one software company has a software product with a regression test suite containing over 30,000 test cases that requires over 1000 machine hours to execute [2]. Hundreds of hours of engineer time are also needed to oversee this regression testing process (eg, setting up test runs, monitoring testing results, and maintaining testing resources such as test cases, oracles, and automation utilities).

Numerous techniques and tools have been proposed and developed to reduce the costs of regression testing and to aid regression testing processes, such as test case prioritization (TCP), regression test selection (RTS), and test suite minimization (TSM). Initially, research on regression testing relied primarily on analytical approaches to assess different techniques (eg, [3, 4]). However, regression testing techniques are heuristics, and to properly understand the tradeoffs and factors that influence testing techniques in practice, empirical studies should be performed. In addition to providing information on tradeoffs among techniques, empirical studies also can aid in understanding the hypotheses that should be tested and the controls that are needed in subsequent studies of humans, which are likely to be more expensive. The importance of empirical studies has been perceived by the software engineering community over the past few decades, and recently empirical evaluations of the proposed techniques or approaches have become an essential component when researchers report their work.

Recent surveys [5–7] provide an overview of regression testing techniques and their empirical evaluations that were published before 2010. These surveys found some general trends about regression testing techniques and areas that need to be improved as well as future directions for this research topic. This chapter provides basic concepts of three regression testing techniques including various data sources that the techniques utilize, different types of techniques, and commonly used evaluation metrics for them. This chapter also summarizes findings from the three surveys and discusses recent advances in those three areas.

Section 2 includes background information about regression testing, and Section 3 presents three regression testing techniques and their overall and recent trends. Section 4 concludes this chapter.

2. BACKGROUND

This section provides background information about regression testing and basic concepts of common regression testing techniques.

Regression testing is the process of testing modified software to ensure its continued quality. Typically, regression testing is performed by reusing test cases developed from testing prior versions of the software system and by creating new test cases that will be used to test new features. Informally, regression testing can be defined as follows. As shown in Fig. 1, let P be a program that has been modified to create a new version P' and let T be a test suite developed for P. In the transition from P to P', the program could have regressed. In other words, a previously verified behavior of P could have turned faulty in P'. Regression testing attempts to validate P' in order to determine whether it has regressed.

The existing test suite, T, provides a natural starting point. In practice, engineers often reuse all of the test cases in T_{all} to test P' after removing obsolete test cases (T_{obs}) that are no longer applicable to P'. However, as software systems grow, the size of the test suite can become too large, thus making it too time consuming and costly to run all the tests. Furthermore, depending on the organization's testing environment and situation, this *retest-all* approach can be very expensive [8].

To address this problem, many researchers have proposed various methods for improving the cost effectiveness of regression testing including RTS, TCP, TSM, and test suite augmentation. The right side of Fig. 1 shows the test cases obtained by applying these techniques. RTS techniques select a subset of test cases from T_{all} to meet some desired criterion, such as discarding test cases ($T_{non-mod}$) that do not execute modified code. TCP techniques reorders test cases in T_{all} to enhance the effectiveness of the test suite, such as fault detection rate. TSM reduces the size of T_{all} by eliminating

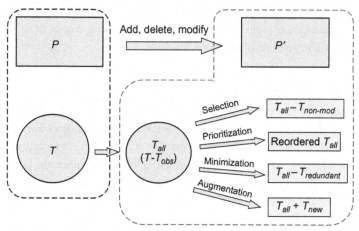

Fig. 1 Regression testing techniques.

redundant test cases ($T_{redundant}$). These three techniques primarily focus on reducing costs by reusing existing test cases. However, in regression testing, in general, simply reusing existing test cases is not sufficient; new test cases also may be required to test new functionality. Test suite augmentation techniques identify newly added code areas and create new test cases (T_{new}) for them.

In this chapter, we focus on the first three regression testing techniques that utilize existing test cases. Formal definitions of these three techniques can be found in the literature survey [7].

3. RECENT ADVANCES IN REGRESSION TESTING TECHNIQUES

This section introduces three regression testing techniques (RTS, TCP, and TSM), and recent advances of these techniques.

Recent surveys on regression testing techniques [5–7] provide a comprehensive understanding of overall trends of the techniques and areas for improvement. Yoo and Harman [7] surveyed 159 papers for all three techniques published between 1977 and 2009 including 87 on RTS, 34 on TSM, and 47 on TCP. Engstrom *et al.* [6] surveyed 27 RTS papers that reported empirical studies published between 1997 and 2006. Catal and Mishra [5] surveyed 120 papers on TCP published between 2001 and 2010. These surveys found that the number of publications on regression testing area continues to grow, and in particular, the area of TCP has rapidly expanded since 2000. They also found that heuristics became diverse including the use of data sources, researchers have paid more attention to empirical evaluations of regression testing techniques over the years, and various application domains have been investigated. The following subsections include more details about each of these techniques.

3.1 Regression Test Selection

RTS techniques (surveyed in [4, 6, 7]) reduce testing costs by selecting a subset of test cases from an existing test suite. RTS techniques use information about P, P', and T to select a subset of T with which to test P'.

A considerable amount of research on RTS techniques has been conducted since 1977 [9], and the number of publications on this area is steadily growing [6, 7]. Early work conducted by Lenung and White [3] and Rothermel and Harrold [10] established a theoretical foundation of RTS techniques and a framework for empirical evaluations of these techniques. Initially, RTS techniques focused on testing procedural languages using source code, but as the program language paradigm shifted to object-oriented languages, and application domains became diverse, various types of RTS techniques were developed.

Safety is an important aspect of RTS techniques. Safe RTS techniques (eg, [11–14]) guarantee that, assuming certain preconditions are met, test cases not selected could not have exposed faults in P' [4]. Informally, these preconditions require that: (1) the test cases in T are expected to produce the same outputs on P' as they did on P; ie, the specifications for these test cases have not changed; and (2) test cases can be executed deterministically, holding all factors that might influence test behavior constant with respect to their states when P was tested with T.

As an example of a safe technique, the graph walk approach, *Dejavu* [13], utilizes control-flow graph representations of the original and modified versions of the program. To select test cases, *Dejavu* performs a synchronous traversal of the control-flow graph (CFG) for P and the control-flow graph (CFG') for P', identifies nodes that that have been added, deleted, or modified from CFG to CFG', and from the test suite for P, selects all tests that reach nodes that are new in, modified for P', and deleted from P. To illustrate this approach, consider Fig. 2 [15] that shows procedure *Avg* and its modified procedure, *Avg'*. The table shows three test cases for *Avg* and test

Graph walking approach

Procedure *Avg*	Procedure *Avg'*
S1 cnt = 0	S1' cnt = 0
S2 fread(fptr,n)	S2' fread(fptr,n)
S3 while (not EOF) do	S3' while (not EOF) do
S4 if (n<0)	S4' if (n<=0)
	S5a print("input error")
S5 return(error)	S5' return(error)
else	else
S6 nums[cnt] = n	S6' nums[cnt] = n
S7 cnt++	S7' cnt++
endif	endif
S8 fread(fptr,n)	S8' fread(fptr,n)
endwhile	endwhile
S9 avg = mean(nums,cnt)	S9' avg = mean(nums,cnt)
S10 return(avg)	S10' return(avg)

Tests and statement coverage for *Avg*

Test	t1	t2	t3
Input	Empty file	−1	1 2 3
Output	0	Error	2
Coverage	s1, s2, s3, s9, s10	s1, s2, s3, s4, s5, s9, s10	s1, s2, s3, s4, s6, s7, s8, s9, s10

Selected Tests = {t2, t3}

Fig. 2 Example of safe regression test selection taken from G. Rothermel, M.J. Harrold, Empirical studies of a safe regression test selection technique, IEEE Trans. Softw. Eng. 24 (6) (1998) 401-419.

traces (statement coverage). Statement *S4* has been modified, and statement *S5a* has been added. *Dejavu* builds CFGs for *Avg* and *Avg'*, walks the two CFGs comparing two corresponding nodes, and identifies nodes that have been changed from the previous version. Using the test coverage information, the approach selects test cases that exercise the changed nodes. In this example, the graph walk approach selects two test cases, t2 and t3, for the modified procedure *Avg'*.

Two other aspects of RTS techniques involve *precision* and *efficiency*. Precision concerns the extent to which techniques correctly deduce that specific test cases do not need to be reexecuted. Efficiency concerns the cost of collecting the data necessary to execute an RTS technique, and the cost of executing that technique. Tradeoffs between precision and efficiency, and their relative cost-benefits vary with characteristics of programs, modifications, and test suites [16].

3.1.1 Data Sources and Techniques

Most of these techniques are code-based and use information about code changes and code coverage to guide the test selection process. Depending on the techniques implemented, in addition to coverage or change information, other data sources (eg, code complexity, code dependency, test granularity, and fault history) have been utilized. Some techniques have used other types of software artifacts, such as requirements specifications, and UML models [17–19]. These techniques are particularly useful when source code is not available to the testers.

Two surveys [6, 7] classified RTS techniques into several classes, and some of the techniques are summarized as follows (for more detailed descriptions and extended discussions about them, see the two surveys):

- Firewall approach: This approach was presented by Leung and White [20] to improve regression testing at the integration level. The approach sets a firewall around the modified modules and the modules related to them, and selects test cases within the firewall. This approach has been applied to a different language paradigm (object-oriented language [21, 22]) and wider application domains (eg, GUI, COTS applications, and distributed software [23–25]).

- Graph walking approach: This approach was presented by Rothermel and Harrold [10, 13, 15], which was already discussed. This approach has been further extended by many researchers in various ways, such as, applying it to different languages (eg, C++, Java, and AspectJ) [12, 26, 27], using various software artifacts (eg, behavior models and requirements/system specifications) [28, 29], and considering wider application domains (eg, component-based systems and web services) [18, 30].

- Data-flow analysis approach: This approach, presented by Harrold and Soffa [31], identifies definition-use pairs of the variables affected by code modification and selects test cases that executes such pairs. Other researchers have improved the effectiveness of test selection by combining the data-flow analysis approach with other techniques, such as the use of slicing techniques, and code coverage-based minimization/prioritization [32, 33].
- Model-based approach: This approach uses models (eg, use cases, class/sequence diagrams, and state models) to select test cases rather than relying on source code information. Briand *et al.* [34] presented an approach that traces the relationship between UML design models and test cases, and selects test cases that affected by design changes. Several other researchers have presented UML model-based test selection approaches that were applied to various application areas, such as telecommunications and component-based applications [35–37].
- Other approaches: Several other techniques that can be applied to RTS include integer programming [9], symbolic execution [38], and slicing [39, 40].

3.1.2 Evaluation Metrics

Initially, RTS techniques have been evaluated analytically by measuring complexity or safety of algorithms, but to properly assess their cost effectiveness in practice, recent research on RTS (and regression testing in general) has employed empirical evaluations.

Because the main goal of RTS techniques is to find a subset of test cases to be rerun, a typical evaluation metric for these techniques is the number of test cases selected or the test case reduction rate. Savings in number of test cases might not be proportional to savings in testing time. For example, all the test cases excluded could be inexpensive while those not excluded could be expensive. Thus, another evaluation metric is the time required to execute the selected subset of the test suite on the modified version of the program. For nonsafe techniques, the selected test cases might lose fault detection abilities. To evaluate these techniques, precision and recall have been used. Precision measures the ratio of selected tests that detect defects, and recall measures the ratio of tests with faults were detected.

Furthermore, RTS techniques have associated costs, and depending on the testing processes employed and other cost factors, they may not reduce overall regression testing costs despite improvements in rates of fault detection. If savings from RTS techniques do not exceed the costs of applying them, no benefits are gained. Therefore, to properly evaluate RTS techniques, some researchers considered tradeoffs between costs and benefits of RTS techniques. For example, Leung and White [41] presented a cost model that considers some of the factors (testing time, technique execution time) that affect the cost of regression testing of a software system. Malishevsky et al. [42] extended this work with cost models for RTS and TCP that incorporate benefits related to omission of faults and rate of fault detection. Do and Rothermel [2, 43] developed a cost-benefit model, the EVOMO (EVOlution-aware economic MOdel for regression testing) model, that helps evaluate regression testing techniques considering costs and benefits across entire system lifetimes. EVOMO involves two equations: one that captures the costs related to the salaries of the engineers who perform regression testing (to translate time spent into monetary values) and one that captures the revenue gains or losses related to changes in the system release time (to translate time-to-release into monetary values). The major cost components that EVOMO captures are as follows: costs for applying regression testing techniques, costs associated with missed faults, costs for artifact analysis, costs of delayed fault detection feedback, and costs associated with obsolete tests.

3.1.3 Recent Advances

This section introduces research about RTS published after 2010. As previously mentioned, in this research area (regression testing in general), application domains and the types of data utilized are diversified, and more researchers consider the practicality of the techniques. Therefore, rather than exhaustively introducing papers published between 2010 and 2015, this section presents recent research that carries the aforementioned trends. The same selection principle applies to TCP and TSM.

Kim et al. [44] presented a RTS technique aimed for ontology-driven database systems because traditional RTS approaches cannot be applied for such systems; changes in ontology systems are typically semantics and descriptions of the data rather than code modifications. The proposed technique builds graphs for the original and modified ontologies. The ontology knowledge consists of two entities: a set of classes that specify the concepts in an application domain and relationships among those classes. The technique compares the two graphs and identifies the changes by collecting three sets of entities: added entities, deleted entities, and entities affected by changes. To select test cases using these entity sets, information about the relationship between tests and entities for the original ontology is required. The information was obtained by parsing the test queries and extracting the terms in each test query. The approach was evaluated using two biomedical ontology-driven database systems in terms of effectiveness and efficiency.

Another recent research conducted by Mirarab [45] introduced a size-constrained regression test selection (SRTS) that selects a subset of test cases with the predetermined size of tests using multicriteria optimization implemented integer linear programming. Unlike existing multiobjective approaches, the research indicated that the multicriteria optimization function tries to achieve a high fault detection rate of the selected test cases. The proposed approach is not safe because it can discard test cases that can detect faults, but this approach can be very practical when the company faces situations under time constraints. In practice, software development processes often impose time constraints on regression testing; therefore this approach can help use limited resources more effectively under such circumstances. The approach was evaluated by applying several RTS techniques (coverage based and Bayesian Network based) to five Java applications.

Qu et al. [46] presented a RTS approach for configurable software systems. The proposed approach selects test cases for the preselected configurations, assuming that there are no changes in source code when testing with different configurations. The approach has four steps: (1) collect configuration differences between two sets of configurations, (2) analyze the impact of configuration changes using program slicing and collects functions that are impacted by the changes, (3) compute the function coverage of test cases, and (4) select test cases that are affected by the changes. The proposed approach was evaluated by using an industrial application, ABB1 which has 129 configurable options distributed among 394 variables. The results of the study indicate that only 20% of test cases are needed to test the new configured system.

Another industrial research conducted by Hemmati and Briand [47] presents a model-based test case selection. This approach computes similarity measures using triggers and guards on transitions of state models and applies a genetic algorithm (GA) to select test cases. The test cases are generated from a state model, and they are abstract tests rather than concrete/executable tests. Because similarity comparisons are completed at the abstract level (hiding unnecessary information), and the executable test cases are generated after selecting abstract tests to be rerun, the cost for test case generation can be reduced. Several similarity functions were used in order to evaluate the proposed approach, such as Counting, Hamming, Jaccard, Levenshtein, Global, and Local, and the best results were compared with common heuristics (random and coverage-based test selection techniques).

3.2 Test Case Prioritization

TCP techniques (eg, [33, 48]) offer an alternative approach to improving regression testing cost effectiveness. These techniques help engineers reveal faults early in testing, which allows them to begin debugging earlier than might otherwise be possible. In this case, entire test suites may still be executed, which avoids the potential drawbacks associated with omitting test cases; achieving greater parallelization of debugging and testing activities results in cost savings. Alternatively, if testing activities are cut short and test cases must be omitted, prioritization can improve the chances that important test cases will be executed. In this case, cost savings related to early fault detection (by those test cases that are executed) still apply, and additional benefits accrue from lowering the number of faults that might otherwise be missed through less appropriate runs of partial test suites.

Depending on the types of information available relating to test cases, various TCP techniques can be utilized. One type of information concerns coverage of code elements, and techniques can be distinguished in terms of the type of code elements used. For example, one technique, *total block coverage prioritization*, simply sorts the test cases in the order of the number of blocks they cover. Fig. 3 shows an example that has four test cases and eight blocks covered by these test cases. In this example, from the original test suite

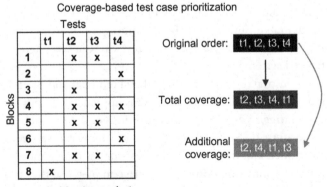

Fig. 3 Test case prioritization techniques.

T, total block coverage prioritization puts t2 first, followed by t3, t4, and t1. The desired outcome in using such a technique is that the ability to reveal a fault will correlate with the size of a test's coverage in the code. From this technique, the selection of t2 first resulted in t3 adding nothing new to the coverage; t3 covers all the same blocks that t2 did. Therefore, another method is to pick tests that yield the most coverage of blocks that were previously uncovered. *Additional block coverage prioritization* iteratively selects a test case that yields the greatest block coverage and then adjusts the coverage information for the remaining test cases to indicate their coverage of blocks not yet covered; this process is repeated until all blocks coverable by at least one test case have been covered. In this example, *additional block coverage prioritization* picks t2 first, followed by t4, t1, and t3.

Because of their appealing benefits in practice, such as flexibility to adjust tests for time and budget constraints, various TCP techniques have been proposed and studied by many researchers and practitioners [7, 8, 49], and many empirical studies have shown the effectiveness of TCP [2, 50].

3.2.1 Data Sources and Techniques

Depending on the types of information available, various TCP techniques can be utilized, but similarly to RTS techniques, the majority of TCP techniques have used source code information to implement prioritization techniques. For instance, many researchers utilized code coverage information to implement prioritization techniques [48, 49, 51], and recent prioritization techniques used other types of code information, such as slices [52], change history [53], or code modification information, and fault proneness of code [54].

Beyond code-based information, other types of software artifacts, such as software requirements and design information, have also been utilized. For example, Srikanth *et al.* [55] proposed a TCP approach using several requirements-related factors, eg, requirements complexity and requirements volatility, for the early detection of severe faults. Krishnamoorthi and Mary [56] also proposed a model to prioritize test cases using the requirements specification to improve the rate of severe fault detection. Arafeen and Do [57] proposed an approach that clusters requirements based on similarities obtained through a text-mining technique and that prioritizes test cases using the requirements-tests relationship. In addition to requirements and design information, some other researchers have used software risk information to prioritize test cases in order to exercise test cases on the code areas with potential risks as early as possible [58, 59].

Two surveys [5, 7] organized TCP techniques into several classes, and some of the techniques are summarized as follows (for more detailed descriptions and extended discussions about them, see the two surveys):

- Code coverage-based approach: This approach is the most widely used and studied TCP approach. Various types of techniques that consider different code component granularity and greedy algorithms have been presented and empirically evaluated including statement/block/ function/method/class coverage, branch coverage, MC/DC (Modified Condition/Decision Coverage), code modification, fault exposing potential, and hill climbing/genetic algorithms [48, 49, 60–63].

- History-based approach: This approach uses history information about software artifacts. Kim et al. [51] presented a technique in which information from previous regression testing cycles is used to better inform the selection of a subset of an existing test suite for use on a modified version of a system. Sherriff et al. [53] utilized change history to gather change impact information and to prioritize test cases accordingly. Carlson et al. [64] presented clustering-based techniques that utilize real fault history information including code coverage.

- Requirements-based approach: This approach uses requirements properties to prioritize test cases. A few researchers have studied the use of requirements during software testing. For example, Srikanth et al. [55] present an approach to prioritizing test cases at the system level using system requirements, and Srivastava et al. [65] utilized requirements information including risk factors involving the requirements. Other researchers presented approaches that consider additional factors, such as factors related to requirement specification (eg, customer priority, requirements changes, or requirements similarity) [56, 57].

- Model-based approach: Korel et al. [66] presented prioritization techniques using system models including information collected during modified model execution. Later, they extended their work to an approach that prioritizes test cases when modifications do not involve changes in models but only in source code [67].

- Human-based approach: Some techniques utilize a human expert's knowledge to improve TCP techniques. For example, Tonella et al. [68] presented a TCP technique that utilizes a user's knowledge using a machine learning algorithm called Case-Based Ranking. Yoo et al. [69] used the Analytic Hierarchy Process to improve TCP techniques by employing expert knowledge, and compared the proposed approach with the conventional coverage-based TCP technique.

- Other approaches: Several other techniques can be applied to TCP, such as interaction [50, 70], probabilistic [54], distribution [71], and cost-aware [72] techniques.

3.2.2 Evaluation Metrics

Because most TCP techniques proposed to date focus primarily on increasing the rate of fault detection of a prioritized test suite, the rate of fault detection is frequently used for evaluating TCP techniques. To measure the rate of fault detection, a metric called APFD (Average Percentage Faults Detected) has been introduced [48, 49]. This metric measures the weighted average of the percentage of faults detected over the life of a test suite. APFD values range from 0 to 100; higher numbers imply faster (better) fault detection rates. More formally, let T be a test suite containing n test cases, and let F be a set of m faults revealed by T. Let TF_i be the first test case in ordering T' of T which reveals fault i. The APFD for test suite T' is given by the equation:

$$APFD = 1 - \frac{TF_1 + TF_2 + \cdots + TF_m}{nm} + \frac{1}{2n}$$

The APFD metric assumes that test costs and fault severities are uniform, but they can vary in practice. $APFD_c$, which is a variation of APFD, accounts for varying test case and fault costs [73]. This metric allows us to properly evaluate TCP techniques when faults have different levels of fault severity and test cases have different execution costs. NAPFD [50] is another variation of APFD. NAPFD considers cases where the rate of fault detection of different size test suites or faults is being compared. In addition to these APFD-based metrics, other metrics have been used. RP (most likely relative position) measures an average relative position of the first failed test [74], and CE (Coverage Effectiveness) incorporates the cost and the coverage of each test case [75]. Furthermore, a few cost models have been used to evaluate TCP techniques as explained in RTS evaluation metrics.

3.2.3 Recent Advances

Haidry and Miller [76] presented an interesting approach that prioritizes functional test cases by analyzing structural dependencies among test cases. The approach reorders test cases based on the complexity of interactions among test cases to increase the fault detection rate. Their work proposes techniques that use two different dependency structures: open and closed dependency structures. For a given dependency between two test cases, t1 and t2, an open dependency structure specifies that t1 should be executed at some point before t2. A closed dependency structure requires that t1 should be executed immediately before t2. Although the system under test is not constructed as a model, this approach is somewhat model based because it does not use code coverage information and it does not need to analyze source code. Instead, this approach constructs dependency structures from test cases, and prioritizes test cases based on the constructed information. One challenge with this approach is to extract test dependencies because such a task requires a good understanding of the system under test and its tests. In the empirical study, an independent test engineer extracted test dependencies. The proposed techniques were evaluated using six applications comparing to several existing prioritization techniques, such as code coverage based, greedy, and random techniques.

Another interesting research conducted by Saha et al. [77] applied an information retrieval approach to TCP. TCP and information retrieval (IR) manipulate different types of software artifacts. TCP uses test cases and source code, and IT uses documents written in natural language). Many documents produced by software engineers are text based, and software developers tend to use meaningful names for comments or identifier names when writing code and also use similar terms when writing test cases for the source code. This means that IR can be utilized in aiding various software engineering tasks. The proposed approach reduces a TCP problem to an IR problem. The program difference between two versions is the query, and the test cases are the document collection. Then, test cases are ranked based on the similarity score between the program differences and test cases. Saha et al. built a prototype, REPiR (Regression test Prioritization using information Retrieval), and evaluated the proposed approach using eight open source applications that are from various application domains, by comparing with several traditional TCP techniques.

A research study conducted by Arafeen and Do [57] investigated the relationship between test cases and requirements to improve test prioritization. Similar or related requirements are typically implemented in the same class or in classes under the same subsystem; therefore test cases associated with a similar or related set of requirements tend to exercise a similar set of classes. Additionally, test cases with common properties tend to have similar fault detection ability. Based on this observation, a TCP technique was proposed that clusters test cases based on requirement similarities. The approach uses a text-mining technique that provides a means to cluster relevant requirements. The requirements are clustered based on the distribution of words that cooccur in the requirements. This process includes three tasks: term extraction, term-document matrix construction, and k-means clustering. Test cases that are associated with requirements in each cluster are identified using the requirement-tests traceability matrix. To prioritize test cases for each cluster, the technique uses a code complexity metric that was calculated using Lines of Code, Nested Block Depth, and McCabe Cyclomatic Complexity. The final step of the approach is to create a set of reordered test cases. To do so, the clusters are prioritized based on the importance of requirements, and the final reordered test cases are created by visiting the prioritized clusters. The approach was evaluated using two Java applications that provided requirements documents by comparing to traditional prioritization techniques that do not use requirements and clustering information.

Staats *et al.* [78] considered a different class of software artifacts, test oracles, to improve TCP. They proposed an approach that utilizes information about test oracles to prioritize test cases. The approach captures data flow information from variable assignments to test oracles from during test execution, and then prioritizes test cases by using the captured data flow information. When prioritizing test cases, this approach tries to minimize the distance from each variable *def* to a *use* in an oracle. The approach was evaluated using three reactive case examples by comparing to two traditional prioritization techniques (random and additional block coverage).

3.3 Test Suite Minimization

As software evolves over time, the number of test cases can grow rapidly; therefore the cost for regression testing and test suite maintenance can become far too costly. Because of the changes in software caused by adding, deleting, and modifying software components, some old test cases cannot be applied to a new version of the program any longer (obsolete test cases), or some test cases produce the same coverage of the program as other test cases (redundant test cases) [79]. *TSM* techniques attempt to reduce the size of test suites by removing these obsolete and redundant test cases. By removing these test cases, engineers can reduce the costs of exercising, validating, and managing these test cases over time [80]. While identifying the minimum set of test cases without altering fault detection abilities would be ideal, the TSM problem is NP-complete [81]; therefore the TSM techniques use heuristics, which produce the approximate minimum test set. Since this technique often is referred to as test suite reduction, minimization and reduction are used interchangeably.

3.3.1 Data Sources and Techniques

The majority of TSM techniques have primarily used code coverage information [79, 82, 83], but other types of information have been utilized, such as graph representations of the system (eg, state models) and data-flow information [84–86].

A survey [7] summarized TSM techniques as follows:

- Code coverage-based approach: Harrold *et al.* [79] presented a technique that selects a representative set of test cases by eliminating redundant and obsolete tests from a set of test requirements, which is based on the minimum hitting set problem. Chen and Lau [82] presented heuristics for the set cover problem, known as GE (select all essential tests, and then select tests from unsatisfied requirements) and GRE (remove redundant tests first, and then apply GE heuristic). Offutt *et al.* [83] presented a technique that reduces the size of a test suite by reordering the test execution sequences. In addition to these aforementioned techniques, many other heuristics have been presented and empirically evaluated, such as heuristics using dynamic information [87, 88], a heuristic that uses branch coverage and data-flow analysis [89], and logic criterion-based heuristics [90].

- Model-based approach: Vaysburg *et al.* [91] presented a technique that uses Extended Finite State Machine (EFSM) dependence analysis to reduce test suites that were generated based on requirements. Korel *et al.* [92] extended this research by incorporating a technique that identifies changes in EFSM models (added/deleted transitions) automatically. Anido *et al.* [93] presented a technique that reduces test cases for embedded systems, in which the systems are represented in Finite State Machines (FSMs).

- Graph-based approach: Marre and Bertolino [84] presented a technique that uses spanning sets of entities for a decision-to-decision graph (ddgraph—a compact version of a regular control flow graph) as a coverage criterion, and identifies a minimum set of tests based on the criterion.

3.3.2 Evaluation Metrics

The primary goal of TSM is to reduce the size of the test suite; therefore the rate of test suite reduction has been used for evaluating TSM techniques. While the size of the test suite is being reduced, fault detection ability or code coverage could be lost. Therefore, in addition to measuring the rate of test suite reduction, fault detection rate or code coverage were used to evaluate TSM techniques. Additionally, algorithms for implementing TSM techniques are more complex than RTS and TCP, so the execution time of the techniques is often used for evaluation.

3.3.3 Recent Advances

While the purpose of the majority of TSM techniques is trying to find a near optimum set of reduced test cases, Hao *et al.* [94] proposed a different approach, which reduces a test suite by allowing test engineers to set a upper limit on loss in fault detection capability (on-demand test suite reduction). By doing this, the approach can control the fault detection capability and can satisfy strict demands on a degree of loss in fault detection capability. After setting certain percentage levels for a upper limit on loss in fault detection capability and a confidence level of the instances where it is applied, the approach selects a representative subset of tests that satisfies the same test requirements as an initial test suite and a given demand (a upper limit on loss in fault detection capability and a confidence level). The proposed approach constructs a fault-detection-loss table by collecting statistics about losses in fault detection capability at the statement level considering three confidence levels (90%, 95%, and 99%). After collecting this information, the approach models on-demand suite reduction as an Integer Linear Programming problem with two ILP models that use local and global constraints. Finally, the approach produces a representative subset by solving the ILP problem. The approach was evaluated using C and Java programs and compared to a traditional approach developed by Harrold *et al.* [79].

Blue *et al.* [95] investigated an interaction-based test suite minimization (ITSM) problem in the industrial context. The approach is based on combinatorial test design (CTD). The CTD approach is effective for various systems types and testing domains, and it works well when the tested functionality depends on multiple factors. Two requirements of CTD prevent it from being applied in practice: (1) CTD requires precisely defined restrictions between the different parameters. This requirement can be problematic when systems have a large number of parameters, and the relationship among parameters is complex; (2) The test suite constructed by CTD requires the implementation of new test cases. While the ITSM approach is complementary to CTD, it addresses cases to which CTD cannot be applied because of those requirements. Instead of constructing a new test suite that satisfies full interaction coverage, ITSM reduces an existing test suite while preserving the interaction coverage. Also, instead of defining restrictions between parameters, ITSM selects a subset of the test suite that preserves its t-wise value combinations. ITSM was evaluated using two real world applications: a healthcare system and a legacy computer terminal interface.

Arlt *et al.* [96] applied TSM to GUI applications. This approach starts with generating test sequences by generalizing test generation algorithms developed from the authors' previous work. Instead of generating test sequences by only considering pairs of def-use events, the generalized algorithm generates all relevant event sequences based on an arbitrary number of dependent events. The number of event sequences generated using the generalized algorithm can be large; in order to address the scalability of the approach, an approach was proposed that uses static analysis based on program slicing to reduce the number of test cases. The approach identifies and eliminates redundant event sequences from GUI test suites using two methods. The first method applies partial order reduction to eliminate event sequences whose execution ordering of first $n-1$ does not affect the final event n. The second method applies causal variable analysis and eliminates event sequences that are causal variable redundant. The approach was evaluated using six open source Java applications.

Gotlieb and Marijan [97] applied a flow network approach to reduce the size of a test suite. They identified three problem areas of test suite reduction, and proposed a new approach that uses network maximum flows to address the existing limitations. The limitations are (1) minimum cardinality test suite is not guaranteed; (2) the existing techniques offer tradeoffs between test reduction time and the number of test cases, but not both; and (3) fault detection capability or code coverage is not preserved. The proposed approach, FLOWER, is an exact method that finds a minimum number of test cases covering the same set of requirements as the original test suite. FLOWER encodes a test suite reduction with a bipartite graph which basically builds the relationship between test requirements and test cases. Based on the graph, FLOWER finds the maximum flows, which produce a subset of a test suite that covers all test requirements, and then a minimum cardinality subset among maximum network flows is found. FLOWER was evaluated using 2000 randomly generated test suite reduction problems which were compared to an Integer Linear Programming approach and a simple greedy approach.

3.4 Additional Remarks on Regression Testing Techniques

In early empirical studies of regression testing techniques, a set of seven small programs known as the Siemens programs [98] and a somewhat larger program, "space," from the European space agency were the primary pro-grams under study (note that the Siemens and space programs have been made available to other researchers since 1999 and have seen widespread use). However, the use of these programs in the empirical studies has been criticized because Siemens and space artifacts present only a small sample of the total population of programs, versions, tests, and faults. Some researchers have also criticized that these programs have been overused in the study of regression testing. The reason that the Siemens and space programs have been popular as experimental artifacts is mainly because these programs have been publicly released for a long period of time, and in the early 2000s, no other shareable software artifacts that were equipped for studies of regression testing techniques existed. Now, the Software-artifact Infrastructure Repos-itory (SIR) [99] that was founded in 2004 provides more diverse types and sizes of software artifacts including automation tools and scripts for supporting empirical studies with software testing and regression testing. Recently, more research is focusing on industrial applications and other open source programs including different types of application domains.

As seen in previous discussions of RTS, TCP, and TSR, early research focused on coverage-based techniques including the "greedy" and the "additional greedy" algorithms. Recently, research has branched out to more diversified and advanced techniques including linear programming, genetic algorithms, and techniques that utilize various types of data sources (eg, code complexity, code dependency, test granularity, fault history, and requirements/design documents). Additionally, more researchers have tried to improve regression testing techniques by incorporating techniques from other areas such as, data mining, machine learning, and information retrieval. It is expected that this trend will continue with growing interests.

4. CONCLUSIONS

This chapter introduced the basic concepts of three widely researched regression testing techniques (RTS, TCP, and TSM), and discussed various data sources that the techniques have utilized, different classes of techniques, and commonly used evaluation metrics for the techniques. This chapter also presented overall trends of the techniques based on the results from three recent surveys and summarized the surveys' findings. Also, recent advances for each area of regression testing techniques were presented.

To date, research in regression testing area continues to grow in many ways as presented in this chapter. However, the surveys suggest methods for improving regression testing, such as developing more model-based techniques, developing techniques that can be practically utilized, and performing more rigorous empirical studies with more publicly available experimental artifacts. While there is some evidence that techniques are being used in practice, it is also noted that there is a gap in technology transfer to industry industry [1]. In order for regression testing techniques and methodologies to be useful in industry and to be transferred faster into practice, they must be developed by considering the context factors related to industrial testing environments and evaluated by using the appropriate assessment methodologies.

REFERENCES

[1] M.J. Harrold, A. Orso, Retesting software during development and maintenance, in: Proceedings of the International Conference on Software Maintenance: Frontiers of Software Maintenance, 2008, pp. 88–108.

[2] H. Do, S. Mirarab, L. Tahvildari, G. Rothermel, The effects of time constraints on test case prioritization: a series of controlled experiments, IEEE Trans. Softw. Eng. 36 (5) (2010). september.

[3] H.K.N. Leung, L. White, Insights into regression testing, in: Proceedings of the Conference on Software Maintenance, 1989, pp. 60–69.

[4] G. Rothermel, M.J. Harrold, Analyzing regression test selection techniques, IEEE Trans. Softw. Eng. 22 (8) (1996) 529–551.

[5] C. Catal, D. Mishra, Test case prioritization: a systematic mapping study, Softw. Qual. J. 21 (2013) 445–478.

[6] E. Engstrom, P. Runeson, M. Skoglund, A systematic review on regression test selection techniques, Inform. Softw. Technol. 52 (1) (2010) 14–30.

[7] S. Yoo, M. Harman, Regression testing minimisation, selection and prioritisation : a survey, 22 (2) (March 2012).

[8] A. Srivastava, J. Thiagarajan, Effectively prioritizing tests in development environment, in: Proceedings of the International Symposium on Software Testing and Analysis, 2002, pp. 97–106.

[9] K. Fischer, A test case selection method for the validation of software maintenance modifications, in: International Computer Software and Applications Conference, 1977, pp. 421–426.

[10] G. Rothermel, M.J. Harrold, A framework for evaluating regression test selection techniques, in: Proceedings of the International Conference on Software Engineering, 1994, pp. 201–210.

[11] Y.F. Chen, D.S. Rosenblum, K.P. Vo, TestTube: a system for selective regression testing, in: Proceedings of the International Conference on Software Engineering, 1994, pp. 211–220.

[12] M.J. Harrold, J. Jones, T. Li, D. Liang, A. Orso, M. Pennings, S. Sinha, S. Spoon, A. Gujarathi, Regression test selection for Java software, in: Proc. Conf. O.-O. Programming, Systems, Langs., and Apps., 2001.

[13] G. Rothermel, M.J. Harrold, A safe, efficient regression test selection technique, ACM Trans. Softw. Eng. Methodol. 6 (2) (1997) 173–210.

[14] F.I. Vokolos, P.G. Frankl, Empirical evaluation of the textual differencing regression testing technique, in: Proceedings of the International Conference on Software Maintenance, 1998, pp. 44–53.

[15] G. Rothermel, M.J. Harrold, Empirical studies of a safe regression test selection technique, IEEE Trans. Softw. Eng. 24 (6) (1998) 401–419.

[16] J. Bible, G. Rothermel, D. Rosenblum, A comparative study of coarse- and fine-grained safe regression test selection techniques, ACM Trans. Softw. Eng. Methodol. 10 (2) (2001) 149–183.

[17] L.C. Briand, Y. Labiche, G. Soccar, Automating impact analysis and regression test selection based on UML design, in: Proceedings of the International Conference on Software Maintenance, 2002, pp. 252–261.

[18] A. Orso, H. Do, G. Rothermel, M.J. Harrold, D. Rosenblum, Using component metadata to regression test component-based software, J. Softw. Test. Verif. Reliab. 17 (2) (2007) 61–94.

[19] A. von Mayrhauser, N. Zhang, Automated regression testing using DBT and Sleuth, J. Softw. Mainten. 11 (2) (1999) 93–116.

[20] H.K.N. Leung, L.J. White, A study of integration testing and software regression at the integration level, in: Proceedings of the Conference on Software Maintenance, 1990, pp. 290–300.

[21] D. Kung, J. Gao, P. Hsia, J. Lin, Y. Toyoshima, Class firewall, test order, and regression testing of object-oriented programs, J. object-oriented programm. 8 (2) (1995) 51–65.

[22] L. White, K. Jaber, B. Robinson, V. Rajlich, Extended firewall for regression testing: an experience report, J. Softw. Mainten. Evol. 20 (6) (2008) 419–433.

[23] L. White, H. Almezen, S. Sastry, Firewall regression testing of gui sequences and their interactions, in: IEEE International Conference on Software Maintenance, 2003, pp. 398–409.

[24] J. Zheng, B. Robinson, L. Williams, K. Smiley, Applying regression test selection for COTS-based applications, in: International Conference on Software Engineering, 2006, pp. 512–522.

[25] M. Skoglund Mi, P. Runeson, A case study of the class firewall regression test selection technique on a large scale distributed software system, in: International Symposium on Empirical Software Engineering and Measurement, 2005, pp. 74–83.

[26] G. Rothermel, M.J. Harrold, J. Dedhia, Regression test selection for C++ programs, J. Softw. Test. Verif. Reliab. 10 (2) (2000) 77–109.

[27] G. Xu, A. Rountev, Regression test selection for AspectJ software, in: International Conference on Software Engineering, 2007, pp. 65–74.

[28] E. Martins, V. Vieira, Regression test selection for testable classes, in: Lecture Notes in Computer Science: Dependable Computing–EDCC, 2005, pp. 453–470.

[29] Y. Chen, R.L. Probert, D.P. Sims, Specification-based regression test selection with risk analysis, in: Proceedings of the 2002 Conference of the Centre for Advanced Studies on Collaborative research, 2002.

[30] M. Ruth, S. Tu, A safe regression test selection technique for web services, in: International Conference on Internet and Web Applications and Services, 2007, pp. 47–52.

[31] M.J. Harrold, M.L. Soffa, An incremental approach to unit testing during maintenance, in: Proceedings of the Conference on Software Maintenance, 1988, pp. 362–367.

[32] R. Gupta, M.J. Harrold, M.L. Soffa, An approach to regression testing using slicing, in: Proceedings of the Conference on Software Maintenance, 1992, pp. 299–308.

[33] W.E. Wong, J.R. Horgan, S. London, H. Agrawal, A study of effective regression testing in practice, in: Proceedings of the International Symposium on Software Reliability Engineering, 1997, pp. 230–238.

[34] L.C. Briand, Y. Labiche, S. He, Automating regression test selection based on UML designs, Inform. Softw. Technol. 51 (2009) 16–30.

[35] Q. Farooq, M. Iqbal, Z. Malik, A. Nadeem, An approach for selective state machine based regression testing, in: International Workshop on Advances in Model-based Testing, 2007, pp. 44–52.

[36] Y. Le Traon, T. Jeron, J. Jezequel, P. Morel, Efficient object-oriented integration and regression testing, IEEE Trans. Reliab. 49 (1) (2000) 12–25.

[37] Y. Wu, J. Offutt, Maintaining evolving component-based software with UML, in: European Conference on Software Maintenance and Reengineering, 2003, pp. 133–142.

[38] S. Yau, Z. Kishimoto, A method for revalidating modified programs in the maintenance phase, in: COMPSAC '87: The Eleventh Annual International Computer Software and Applications Conference, 1987, pp. 272–277.

[39] H. Agrawal, J. Horgan, E. Krauser, S. London, Incremental regression testing, in: Proceedings of the Conference on Software Maintenance, 1993, pp. 348–357.

[40] S. Bates, S. Horwitz, Incremental program testing using program dependence graphs, in: Proceedings of the 20th ACM Symposium on Principles of Programming Languages, 1993, pp. 384–396.

[41] H.K.N. Leung, L.J. White, A cost model to compare regression test strategies, in: Proceedings of the Conference on Software Maintenance, 1991.

[42] A. Malishevsky, G. Rothermel, S. Elbaum, Modeling the cost-benefits tradeoffs for regression testing techniques, in: IEEE International Conference on Software Maintenance, 2002, pp. 204–213.

[43] H. Do, G. Rothermel, An empirical study of regression testing techniques incorporating context and lifecycle factors and improved cost-benefit models, in: Proceedings of the ACM SIGSOFT Symposium on Foundations of Software Engineering, 2006.

[44] M. Kim, J. Cobb, M.J. Harrold, T. Kurc, A. Orso, J. Saltz, A. Post, K. Malhotra, S. Navathe, Efficient regression testing of ontology-driven systems, in: International Symposium on Software Testing and Analysis, 2012, pp. 320–330.

[45] S. Mirarab, S. Akhlaghi, L. Tahvildari, Size-constrained regression test case selection using multicriteria optimization, IEEE Trans. Softw. Eng. 38 (4) (2012) 936–956.

[46] X. Qu, M. Acharya, B. Robinson, Impact analysis of configuration changes for test case selection, in: International Symposium on Software Reliability Engineering, 2011, pp. 140–149.

[47] H. Hemmati, L. Briand, An industrial investigation of similarity measures for model-based test case selection, in: International Symposium on Software Reliability Engineering, 2010, pp. 141–150.

[48] G. Rothermel, R. Untch, C. Chu, M.J. Harrold, Prioritizing test cases for regression testing, IEEE Trans. Softw. Eng. 27 (10) (2001) 929–948.

[49] S. Elbaum, A.G. Malishevsky, G. Rothermel, Test case prioritization: a family of empirical studies, IEEE Trans. Softw. Eng. 28 (2) (2002) 159–182.

[50] X. Qu, M. Cohen, G. Rothermel, Configuration-aware regression testing: an empirical study of sampling and prioritization, in: Proceedings of the International Conference on Software Testing and Analysis, 2008, pp. 75–86.

[51] J. Kim, A. Porter, A history-based test prioritization technique for regression testing in resource constrained environments, in: Proceedings of the International Conference on Software Engineering, 2002.

[52] D. Jeffrey, N. Gupta, Test case prioritization using relevant slices, in: Int'l Comp. Soft. Appl. Conf., 2006, pp. 411–420.

[53] M. Sherriff, M. Lake, L. Williams, Prioritization of regression tests using singular value decomposition with empirical change records, in: Proceedings of the International Symposium on Software Reliability Engineering, 2007, pp. 81–90.

[54] S. Mirarab, L. Tahvildari, A prioritization approach for software test cases on Baysian Networks, in: Found. A,pp. Softw. Eng., 2007, pp. 276–290.

[55] H. Srikanth, L. Williams, J. Osborne, System test case prioritization of new and regression test cases, in: Proceedings of the International Symposium on Empirical Software Engineering, 2005, pp. 64–73.
[56] R. Krishnamoorthi, S.A. Sahaaya, M. Arul, Factor oriented requirement coverage based system test case prioritization of new and regression test cases, Inform. Softw. Technol. 51 (4) (2009) 799–808.
[57] M. Arafeen, H. Do, Test case prioritization using requirements-based clustering, in: International Conference on Software Testing, Verification and Validation, 2013, pp. 312–321.
[58] H. Stallbaum, A. Metzger, K. Pohl, An Automated Technique for Risk-based Test Case Generation and Prioritization, in: Proceedings of the 3rd International Workshop on Automation of Software Test, 2008, pp. 67–70.
[59] C.S. Hettiarachchi, H. Do, B. Choi, Effective regression testing using requirements and risks, in: Eighth International Conference on Software Security and Reliability, 2014, pp. 157–166.
[60] J. Jones, M.J. Harrold, Test suite reduction and prioritization for modified condition/decision coverage, IEEE Trans. Softw. Eng. 29 (3) (2003) 193–209.
[61] H. Do, G. Rothermel, A. Kinneer, Prioritizing JUnit test cases: an empirical assessment and cost-benefits analysis, Empir. Softw. Eng. Int. J. 11 (1) (2006) 33–70.
[62] Z. Li, M. Harman, R. Hierons, Search algorithms for regression test case prioritization, IEEE Trans. Softw. Eng. 33 (4) (2007) 225–237.
[63] G. Rothermel, R.H. Untch, C. Chu, M.J. Harrold, Test case prioritization: an empirical study, in: Int'l. Conf. Softw. Maint., 1999, pp. 179–188.
[64] R. Carlson, H. Do, A. Denton, A clustering approach to improving test case prioritization: an industrial case study, in: IEEE International Conference on Software Maintenance, 2011, pp. 382–391.
[65] P. Srivastava, K. Kumar, G. Raghurama, Test case prioritization based on requirements and risk factors, Softw. Eng. Notes 33 (4) (2008) 1–5.
[66] B. Korel, L. Tahat, M. Harman, Test prioritization using system models, in: Proceedings of the International Conference on Software Maintenance, 2005, pp. 559–568.
[67] B. Korel, G. Koutsogiannakis, L. Tahat, Application of system models in regression test suite prioritization, in: Proceedings of the International Conference on Software Maintenance, 2008, pp. 247–256.
[68] P. Tonella, P. Avesani, A. Susi, Using the case-based ranking methodology for test case prioritization, in: IEEE International Conference on Software Maintenance, IEEE, 2006, pp. 123–133.
[69] S. Yoo, M. Harman, P. Tonella, A. Susi, Clustering test cases to achieve effective and scalable prioritisation incorporating expert knowledge, in: Proceedings of the International Conference on Software Testing and Analysis, 2009, pp. 201–212.
[70] R. Bryce, C. Colbourn, Prioritized interaction testing for pair-wise coverage with seeding and constraints, J. Inform. Softw. Technol. 48 (10) (2006) 960–970.
[71] D. Leon, A. Podgurski, A comparison of coverage-based and distribution-based techniques for filtering and prioritizing test cases, in: Proceedings of the International Symposium on Software Reliability Engineering, 2003, pp. 442–453.
[72] A. Walcott, M.L. Soffa, G.M. Kapfhammer, R.S. Roos, Time-aware test suite prioritization, in: Proceedings of the International Conference on Software Testing and Analysis, 2006, pp. 1–12.
[73] S. Elbaum, A. Malishevsky, G. Rothermel, Incorporating varying test costs and fault severities into test case prioritization, in: Proceedings of the 23rd International Conference on Software Engineering, IEEE Computer Society, 2001, pp. 329–338.

[74] B. Korel, G. Koutsogiannakis, Experimental comparison of code-based and model-based test prioritization, in: IEEE International Conference on Software Testing Verification and Validation Workshop, 2009, pp. 77–84.

[75] G. Kapfhammer, M.L. Soffa, Using coverage effectiveness to evaluate test suite prioritizations, in: International Workshop on Empirical Assessment of Software Engineering Languages and Technologies, 2007, pp. 19–20.

[76] S. Haidry, T. Miller, Using dependency structures for prioritization of functional test suites, IEEE Trans. Softw. Eng. 39 (2) (2013) 258–275.

[77] R. Saha, L. Zhang, S. Khurshid, D. Perry, An information retrieval approach for regression test prioritization based on program changes, in: International Conference on Software Engineering, 2015, pp. 268–279.

[78] M. Staats, P. Loyola, G. Rothermel, Oracle-centric test case prioritization, in: International Symposium on Software Reliability Engineering, 2012, pp. 311–320.

[79] M.J. Harrold, R. Gupta, M.L. Soffa, A methodology for controlling the size of a test suite, ACM Trans. Softw. Eng. Methodol. 2 (3) (1993) 270–285.

[80] G. Rothermel, M.J. Harrold, J. Ostrin, C. Hong, An empirical study of the effects of minimization on the fault detection capabilities of test suites, in: Proceedings of the International Conference on Software Maintenance, 1998, pp. 34–43.

[81] M.R. Garey, D.S. Johnson, Computers and Intractability, W.H. Freeman, New York, 1979.

[82] T.Y. Chen, M.F. Lau, Dividing strategies for the optimization of a test suite, Inform Process. Lett. 60 (3) (1996) 135–141.

[83] J. Pan J. Offutt, J.M. Voas, Procedures for reducing the size of coverage-based test sets, in: Proc. Int'l. Conf. Testing Comp. Softw., 1995, pp. 111–123.

[84] M. Marre, A. Bertolino, Using spanning sets for coverage testing, IEEE Trans. Softw. Eng. 29 (11) (2003) 974–984.

[85] J.R. Horgan, S.A. London, ATAC: a data flow coverage testing tool for C, in: Proceedings of the Symp. on Assessment of Quality Software Dev. Tools, 1992, pp. 2–10.

[86] P. Schroeder, B. Korel, Black-box test reduction using input-output analysis, in: International Symposium on Software Testing and Analysis, 2000, pp. 173–177.

[87] M. Harder, J. Mellen, M. Ernst, Improving test suites via operational abstraction, in: Proc. 25rd International Conference on Software Eng., 2003, pp. 60–71.

[88] S. McMaster, A. Memon, Call-stack coverage for gui test suite reduction, IEEE Trans. Softw. Eng. 34 (1) (2008) 99–115.

[89] D. Jeffrey, N. Gupta, Test suite reduction with selective redundancy, in: IEEE International Conference on Software Maintenance, 2005, pp. 549–558.

[90] G. Kaminski, P. Ammann, Using logic criterion feasibility to reduce test set size while guaranteeing fault detection, in: International Conference on Software Testing, Verification and Validation, 2009, pp. 356–365.

[91] B. Vaysburg, L. Tahat, B. Korel, Dependence analysis in reduction of requirement based test suites, in: International Symposium on Software Testing and Analysis, 2002, pp. 107–111.

[92] B. Korel, L.H. Tahat, B. Vaysburg, Model based regression test reduction using dependence analysis, in: International Conference on Software Maintenance, 2002, pp. 214–223.

[93] R. Anido, A. Cavalli, L. Lima, N. Yevtushenko, Test suite minimization for testing in context, J. Softw. Test. Verif. Reliab. 13 (3) (2003) 141–155.

[94] D. Hao, L. Zhang, X. Wu, H. Mei, G. Rothermel, On-demand test suite reduction, in: International Conference on Software Engineering, 2012, pp. 738–748.

[95] D. Blue, I. Segall, R. Tzoref-Brill, A. Zlotnick, Interaction-based test-suite minimization, in: International Conference on Software Engineering, 2013, pp. 182–191.

[96] S. Arlt, A. Podelski, M. Wehrle, Reducing gui test suites via program slicing, in: International Symposium on Software Testing and Analysis, 2014, pp. 270–281.

[97] A. Gotlieb, D. Marijan, Flower: optimal test suite reduction as a network maximum flow, in: International Symposium on Software Testing and Analysis, 2014, pp. 171–180.

[98] M. Hutchins, H. Foster, T. Goradia, T. Ostrand, Experiments on the effectiveness of dataflow- and controlflow-based test adequacy criteria, in: Proc. Int'l. Conf. Softw. Eng., 1994, pp. 191–200.

[99] H. Do, S. Elbaum, G. Rothermel, Supporting controlled experimentation with testing techniques: an infrastructure and its potential impact, Int. J. Emp. Softw. Eng. 10 (4) (2005) 405–435.

ABOUT THE AUTHOR

Hyunsook Do is an associate professor in the Department of Computer Science and Engineering at University of North Texas in United States. She received the Ph.D. in Computer Science from University of Nebraska-Lincoln, the M.S. in Computer Science from Tokyo Institute of Technology in Japan, and a B.S. in Computer Science from Sungshin Women's University in South Korea. Her research interests lie in software engineering, particularly software testing and empirical methodologies.

CHAPTER FOUR

Coverage-Based Software Testing: Beyond Basic Test Requirements

W. Masri, F.A. Zaraket
American University of Beirut, Beirut, Lebanon

Contents

Advances in Computers, Volume 103
ISSN 0065-2458
http://dx.doi.org/10.1016/bs.adcom.2016.04.003

Abstract

Code coverage is one of the core quality metrics adopted by software testing practitioners nowadays. Researchers have devised several coverage criteria that testers use to assess the quality of test suites. A *coverage criterion* operates by: (1) defining a set of *test requirements* that need to be satisfied by the given test suite and (2) computing the percentage of the satisfied requirements, thus yielding a quality metric that quantifies the potential adequacy of the test suite at revealing program defects. What differentiates one coverage criterion from another is the set of test requirements involved. For example, *function coverage* is concerned with whether every function in the program has been called, and *statement coverage* is concerned with whether every statement in the program has executed.

The use of code coverage in testing is not restricted to assessing the quality of test suites. For example, researchers have devised test suite minimization and test case generation techniques that also leverage coverage.

Early coverage-based software testing techniques involved basic test requirements such as functions, statements, branches, and predicates, whereas recent techniques involved (1) test requirements that are complex code constructs such as paths, program dependences, and information flows or (2) test requirements that are not necessarily code constructs such as program properties and user-defined test requirements. The focus of this chapter is to compare these two generations of techniques in regard to their effectiveness at revealing defects. The chapter will first present preliminary background and definitions and then describe impactful early coverage techniques followed by selected recent work.

1. INTRODUCTION

For most software programs, the number of potential test cases exercising different program behaviors is practically infinite, which makes exhaustive testing infeasible. Alternatively, the testing community believes that effective use of coverage criteria provides informal assurance that the software program is reliable, ie, contains no defects. That is, coverage criteria provide practical rules for how to select tests and when to stop testing [1].

Researchers devised coverage criteria that testers use to assess the quality of test suites. A *coverage criterion* operates by: (1) defining a set of *test requirements* that need to be satisfied by the given test suite; and (2) computing the percentage of the satisfied requirements, thus yielding a quality metric that quantifies the potential adequacy of the test suite at revealing program defects. What differentiates one coverage criterion from another is the set of test requirements involved. For example, *function coverage* is concerned with whether every function in the program has been called, and *statement coverage* is concerned with whether every statement in the program has executed.

Primarily, testers leverage coverage criteria and configure their coverage requirements to maintain test suites for the purpose of: (1) fully exercising the intended functionality of the system under test (ie, validation testing); (2) guarding against previously detected defects (ie, regression testing); and (3) increasing the likelihood of detecting undiscovered defects (defect testing).

The use of coverage in testing is not restricted to assessing the quality of test suites. As described in later sections, researchers devised test case generation and test suite minimization techniques that leverage coverage.

This chapter is organized as follows. Section 2 provides definitions relevant to coverage-based software testing. Sections 3–5, respectively, describe early work involving basic coverage criteria, advanced coverage criteria, and profiling for basic coverage. Sections 6–12 present more recent work as follows: (a) Section 6 describes an approach for efficient path profiling; (b) Section 7 describes test case generation techniques for path coverage; (c) advanced coverage-based test suite minimization techniques are described in Sections 8 and 9; (d) Section 10 describes PBCOV, a property-based coverage criterion; and (e) Section 11 describes UCov, a user-defined coverage criterion for test case intent verification. Finally, Section 12 concludes.

2. DEFINITIONS

This section provides definitions for entities relevant to the concepts of testing and code coverage. When appropriate, terminology used in Refs. [1,2] will be adopted hereafter.

Definition—Program element: *A program element (pe)* is a programming unit such as a statement, a branch, a def-use pair, or a predicate. Program elements, which could vary considerably in terms of their complexity, are typically derived from control flow, data flow, or logic program constructs.

Definition—Program, test case, and test suite: A *program* (*P*) is a list of statements whose execution describes a set of intended behaviors. A program typically has a set of inputs (*I*) and its execution on one of the inputs $P(i)$, where $i \in I$ defines a program behavior. A test case *t* defines an input of the program and relates it to an expected intended behavior (as determined by an *oracle*). A failure occurs when the behavior of a program on a test case does not match the expected behavior. A test suite *T* is a set of test cases.

Definition—Test requirement: A *test requirement* (*tr*) is a program element that a test case must satisfy or cover. A set of test requirements are denoted as *TR*.

Definition—Coverage criterion: A *coverage criterion* (*C*) is a rule that imposes test requirements *TR* on a test suite *T* and a program *P*. That is, *T* satisfies *C* if and only if every test requirement in *TR* is covered by the execution of *P* over at least one test case in *T*.

Definition—Coverage level: Given a set of test requirements *TR* associated with coverage criterion *C*, a test suite *T*, and a program *P*, the *coverage level* is the ratio of the number of test requirements covered by *T* to the size of *TR*. Note that the coverage level should be at 100% for *T* to satisfy *C*.

Definition—Criteria subsumption: A coverage criterion *C1* *subsumes* *C2* if and only if every test suite that satisfies *C1* also satisfies *C2*. Bear in mind that it is customary to compare coverage criteria in terms of their subsumption relations, and it is generally harder to satisfy *C1* than *C2*, if *C1* subsumes *C2*.

3. EARLY TECHNIQUES: BASIC COVERAGE CRITERIA

Coverage criteria aim at assessing test suite quality. The discussion in this section will be limited to early coverage criteria which require basic program elements to be covered, or equivalently, basic test requirements to be satisfied. We consider a program element to be *basic* if it is *simple* in regard to syntax. While acknowledging that the following is a subjective categorization, we consider the following program elements to be basic: functions, function pairs, statements (or basic blocks), branches, predicates, and clauses (ie, predicates with no logical operators).

3.1 Function Coverage and Function-Pair Coverage

A static call graph captures the potential calling relationships between functions in a program. In such a graph, a node represents a function and an edge *foo* → *bar* indicates that function *foo* might call function *bar* during execution.

The *function coverage criterion* defines *TR* to include all the nodes in the static call graph. Thus, for test suite *T* to satisfy *function coverage*, *T* should execute every function in the program at least once.

The *function-pair coverage criterion* defines *TR* to include all the edges in the static call graph. Therefore, for *T* to satisfy *function-pair coverage*, *T* should induce every potential function invocation in the program at least once.

It is worth mentioning that the exact static call graph is an undecidable problem. This is basically because the computable static call graphs may contain call pairs that might never occur in actual executions of the program. Therefore, the call graphs used when computing the metrics for function–pair coverage are actually over-approximations, thus yielding potentially inaccurate values.

3.2 Statement Coverage and Basic Block Coverage

Control flow is a relation that describes the possible flow of execution in a program. A *control flow graph* (CFG) is a directed graph in which each node represents a statement and each edge represents the flow of control between statements within a function. That is, a CFG captures all paths that might be traversed during the execution of a function. A *SystemCFG* combines all the CFGs of a program by adding an edge to represent each function invocation.

The *statement coverage criterion* defines *TR* to include all the nodes in the SystemCFG. Thus, for *T* to satisfy *statement coverage*, *T* should execute every statement in the program at least once.

A *basic block* is a sequence of consecutive statements in which the flow of control enters at the beginning and leaves at the end without halt or possibility of branching except at the end. CFGs and SystemCFGs are typically built based on basic blocks as opposed to statements. This is widely practiced because the resulting CFGs would be more compact (allowing for more efficient analyses), meanwhile preserving the same control flow information. Consequently, many testers choose to adopt *basic block coverage* as opposed to statement coverage.

Keep in mind that if a test suite *T* exhibits a coverage level of 100% for statement coverage, it will also exhibit 100% for basic block coverage (and vice versa). However, if the coverage level was less than 100% for statement coverage, say 90%, it will not necessarily be 90% for basic block coverage (and vice versa).

3.3 Branch Coverage

The *branch coverage criterion* defines *TR* to include all the branches (edges originating from decision nodes) in all the CFGs of the functions in the subject program. Thus, for *T* to satisfy *branch coverage*, *T* should exercise each branch of each control structure. For example, given an *if* statement, the body of the *if* should be executed in at least one instance and skipped in at least one other instance. Given an *if-else*, the body of the *if* should be executed in at least one instance and the body of the *else* executed in at least one other instance. And given a loop, it should iterate one or more times in at least one instance and zero times in at least one other instance.

3.4 Basic Logic Coverage

This section introduces the three basic *logic coverage criteria*, ie, *predicate coverage*, *clause coverage*, and *combinatorial coverage*. In the context of a conditional program statement, a *predicate* is a Boolean expression whose outcome decides which branch the execution path will follow. For example, given the snippet of Java code below:

```
if ( (x != 1) || (x > y) ) {
    s1: . . .
    } else {
    s2: . . .
    }
```

The Boolean outcome of predicate $((x \;!= 1) \;||\; (x > y))$ will determine whether s_1 or s_2 will execute. A predicate is composed of one or more clauses separated by logical operators (*and, or, not*), where a *clause* is a Boolean expression with no logical operators but possibly relational operators ($>, <, !=$, etc.). In the above example the predicate is composed of the two clauses $(x \;!= 1)$ and $(x > y)$ separated by the logical operator "$||$."

The *predicate coverage criterion* defines *TR* to include all the predicates *p* in the program, and for each *p* to evaluate to *true* and *false*, at least once.

The *clause coverage criterion* defines *TR* to include all the clauses *c* in the program, and for each *c* to evaluate to *true* and *false*, at least once.

Neither of predicate coverage or clause coverage subsumes the other. For example, considering our example and the test cases in the table below, test suite $T1 = \{t1, t2\}$ satisfies predicate coverage but not clause coverage, and test suite $T2 = \{t2, t3\}$ satisfies clause coverage but not predicate coverage.

Test Case(x, y)	(x != 1)	(x > y)	((x != 1) || (x > y))
t1(1, 1)	F	F	F
t2(1, 0)	F	T	T
t3(2, 3)	T	F	T
t4(2, 1)	T	T	T

Test suite $T3 = \{t1, t4\}$ satisfies predicate coverage and clause coverage. However, it is not very effective at covering the various behaviors of the program since both clauses take on the same values in each of $t1$ and $t4$. Clearly, testing the program with all four test cases, ie, inducing all combinations of the clauses, would better cover the various program behaviors. This is what combinatorial coverage calls for.

The *combinatorial coverage criterion* requires that the clauses for each predicate in the program evaluate to each possible combination of truth values. Not only combinatorial coverage subsumes predicate coverage and clause coverage, but it is also considered to be the most effective among logic coverage criteria. However, it is difficult and costly to satisfy when the number of clauses n in a given predicate p exceeds 4 or 5, since 2^n test cases need to be generated just to satisfy the metric for p.

4. EARLY TECHNIQUES: ADVANCED COVERAGE CRITERIA

Here we present early and advanced coverage criteria, namely, def–use pair coverage and active clause coverage. The latter provides the basis for compliance of safety critical avionics software in commercial aircraft as set by the US Federal Aviation Administration (FAA).

4.1 Def-Use Pair Coverage

A statement is *data dependent* on another statement if the latter defines a memory location and the former uses it. Modeling data dependences between statements requires associating two sets of variables with each statement: the set of variables $D(s)$ defined (ie, assigned a value) at s, and the set of variables $U(s)$ used (ie, referenced) at s.

Definition—Let s_1 and s_2 be two statements in a program. s_2 is *data depen-dent* on s_1, if and only if there is a sequence of statements S connecting s_1 to s_2 such that:

$$(D(s_1) \cap U(s_2)) - D(S) \neq 0$$

That is, s_1 defines a variable used at s_2, and there exists a path (in the SystemCFG) from s_1 to s_2 in which that variable is not redefined (killed), ie, there exists a *def-clear path* from s_1 to s_2.

Definition—A definition-use pair or DU pair is a triple $\langle v, d, u \rangle$, where d is a definition of v, u is a use of v, and there is at least a def-clear path from d to u. Researchers have recognized three main variations of definition-use pair coverage, namely, *all-defs coverage*, *all-uses coverage*, and *all-du-paths* coverage.

The *all-defs coverage* requires that each definition reaches at least one use. The *all-uses coverage* requires that each definition reaches all possible uses. The *all-du-paths* coverage requires that each definition reaches all possible uses through all possible def-clear paths. These three variations are illustrated in Fig. 1. The snippet of code in Fig. 1A involves one definition of variable x at statement s_0 and two uses at s_3 and s_4. A single test case that induces executing trace $\langle s_0, s_2, s_4 \rangle$ suffices to satisfy all-defs coverage since it only requires that each definition reaches one use. And given that all-uses coverage is satisfied by having each definition reaching all possible uses, the two test cases inducing executing traces $\langle s_0, s_2, s_3 \rangle$ and $\langle s_0, s_2, s_4 \rangle$ would

A	B

s_0: x = ...;
    if (...) {
s_1:   ...
    }
    else {
s_2:   ...
    }
    if (...) {
s_3:   f(x);
    }
    else {
s_4:   g(x);
    }
	All-defs:
	$\langle s_0, s_2, s_4 \rangle$
	
	All-uses:
	$\langle s_0, s_2, s_3 \rangle$
	$\langle s_0, s_2, s_4 \rangle$
	
	All-du-paths:
	$\langle s_0, s_2, s_3 \rangle$
	$\langle s_0, s_1, s_3 \rangle$
	$\langle s_0, s_2, s_4 \rangle$
	$\langle s_0, s_1, s_4 \rangle$

x is defined at s_0 and used at s_3 and s_4	Possible test execution traces needed to satisfy each of the three criteria

Fig. 1 Example illustrating the three def-use coverage criteria.

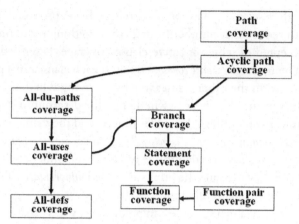

Fig. 2 Structural coverage criteria subsumption.

satisfy this coverage criterion. Finally, all-du-paths coverage requires four test cases since all four def-clear paths from s_0 to s_3 and s_4 need to be executed.

Fig. 2 shows the subsumption hierarchy between the structural coverage criteria presented so far. It also includes *path coverage* and *acyclic path coverage* which will be discussed later in the chapter. The figure shows that (1) all-du-paths coverage subsumes all-uses coverage, which subsumes all-defs coverage and branch coverage; (2) branch coverage subsumes statement coverage, which in turn subsumes function coverage; and (3) function-pair coverage subsumes function coverage. It goes without saying that the subsumption relation is transitive; eg, branch coverage subsumes function coverage and all-du-paths subsumes statement coverage.

Finally, it is important to mention that def-use coverage is complicated by the fact the test requirements cannot be easily and accurately determined. This task involves using static analysis to identify for each definition: (1) all its potential uses in the SystemCFG; and (2) all the def-clear paths reaching each of its uses. Thus requiring the forward traversal of the SystemCFG multiple times starting from each definition. The resulting *TR* is a safe solution (ie, it contains all potential def-use pairs and associated def-clear paths) but might include unsatisfiable test requirements since some of the identified def-clear paths might not be feasible.

4.2 Active Clause Coverage

As stated earlier in Section 3.4, combinatorial coverage is costly and hard to satisfy due to the large number of test cases that need to be generated for each predicate with n clauses. Testing researchers have proposed numerous approaches to reduce that number from 2^n to something more manageable. The most accepted of which is active clause coverage, described next.

The idea behind *active clause coverage* is to test each clause c in a predicate p independently from the other clauses in p by verifying whether c affects the outcome of p; specifically, to verify whether c is the determining factor in the value of p. Informally, if the value of c is flipped and the value of p changes, we say that "c *determines* p" or "c *is active.*" To satisfy active clause coverage, each clause must be shown to determine p. The clause under consideration is called the *major clause* in p, and the others are called *minor clauses*. The concept of *determination* is formalized below.

Definition—Given a major clause c_i in predicate p, we say that c_i *determines* p if the minor clauses $c_j \in p$, $j \neq i$ have values so that changing the truth value of c_i changes the truth value of p.

Several variations of active clause coverage criteria have been proposed, but the most widely used is the *restricted active clause coverage criterion* also known in the industry as *MC/DC* (*Modified Condition/Decision Coverage*), which is required by the FAA for safety critical software.

The *restricted active clause coverage criterion* is formally defined as follows: for each predicate p and each major clause c_i in p, choose values for minor clauses c_j, $j \neq i$, so that c_i determines p. *TR* has two requirements for each c_i: c_i evaluates to *true* and c_i evaluates to *false*. The values chosen for the minor clauses c_j must be the same when c_i is *true* as when c_i is *false*.

The table below illustrates this criterion using predicate $p = (c1 \ \&\&\ c2 \ \&\&\ c3)$. Clause $c1$ determines p (ie, $c1$ is active) due to test cases $\{t1, t5\}$, since a change in the value of $c1$ causes a change in the value of p, while $c2$ and $c3$ are unchanged. Clause $c2$ determines p due to test cases $\{t1, t3\}$, since a change in $c2$ causes a change in p, while $c1$ and $c3$ are unchanged. Similarly for $c3$, it determines p due to test cases $\{t1, t2\}$, while $c1$ and $c2$ are unchanged. Consequently, test suite $\{t1, t2, t3, t5\}$, shown at the bottom of the table, satisfies the *restricted active clause coverage criterion* or *MC/DC*.

Test Case	c1	c2	c3	c1 && c2 && c3
t1	True	True	True	True
t2	True	True	False	False
t3	True	False	True	False
t4	True	False	False	False

t5	False	True	True	False
t6	False	True	False	False
t7	False	False	True	False
t8	False	False	False	False

t1	True	True	True	True
t5	False	True	True	False
t3	True	False	True	False
t2	True	True	False	False

Finally, there are several logic coverage criteria proposed by the research community, of which we only presented four. In regard to subsumption, those are related as follows: combinatorial coverage subsumes active clause coverage, which in turn subsumes clause coverage and predicate coverage.

5. EARLY TECHNIQUES: PROFILING FOR BASIC COVERAGE

Applying any given coverage-based technique requires the use of a profiling tool that enables collecting execution profiles during test suite execution. Such profiles (one per test case) capture the frequency of execution of the program elements associated with the technique at hand. This section briefly describes the approaches adopted by the tools that capture profiles of basic elements, namely, functions, function pairs, basic blocks, branches, def–uses, predicates, and clauses. Section 6 presents an approach for profiling acyclic paths. Detailed descriptions of profiling dependence chains, slice pairs, information flow pairs, and values of variables can be found in Refs. [3–10].

Profiling involves inserting probes in the subject program via instrumentation, which could be carried out at different language levels. For example, some tools instrument the Java or C code, others the Java Byte Code (eg, using BCEL [11] or ASM [12]), and some instrument the binary code (eg, using Pin [13]). Typically, probes are calls to profiler functions that collectively track the occurrence of program events that are of interest to the technique, such as branch executions.

5.1 Profiling Structural Elements

To capture *function profiles*, a probe is inserted at the entry of every function for the purpose of registering the invocation of the given function. This could be achieved by calling a profiler function and passing it a unique identifier of the invoked function, eg, class name, method name, and method signature in the case of Java. Profiling *function pairs* would additionally require that the previously invoked function be taken into consideration.

An important point to make is that for multi-threaded subject programs, the events tracked by the profiler must be labeled with the current thread identifier. This might not be relevant for function or statement profiles, but it is critical for function pair, branch, and def-use pair profiles since each of their profiling elements involves more than a single recorded event.

As noted in Section 3.2, basic block profiles are more widely used than statement profiles. To collect *basic block profiles*, a call to a profiler function is typically inserted at the entry of every basic block. The function is passed a unique identifier of the executed basic block, which comprises the method identifier and the basic block's sequential order within the method.

A program branch is defined by a pair of basic blocks where the first is a decision basic block, ie, having a decision statement as a last statement. Branch profiling tools typically start by building the basic block based CFGs of the profiled functions, which inherently have information about whether a given basic block is a decision basic block or not. Therefore, not all edges in the CFGs are relevant, but only those originating from decision nodes. *Branch profiles* are collected by: (1) inserting a call to a profiler function at the entry of every basic block; (2) considering that a branch was taken if the previously executed basic block is a decision node; and (3) recording the occurrence of a branch by denoting its source and destination basic blocks.

In Section 4.1 we stated that computing TR for def-use coverage is nontrivial. In regard to profiling, all-defs coverage and all-uses coverage are straightforward, but it is not the case for all-du-paths coverage. Since all-du-paths coverage requires tracking specific paths (although simple paths), whereas all-defs coverage and all-uses coverage only require determining whether some set of def-uses occurred regardless of how a definition reached its use(s). We now describe a profiling approach that identifies the set of def-use pairs that occurred during the execution of a test case, that is, an approach that supports all-defs coverage, all-uses coverage, and the coverage-based test suite minimization techniques described in Sections 8 and 9. The approach uses a hash table in which the keys represent unique identifiers of defined variables, and the values represent unique identifiers of the corresponding definition statements. That is, the table tracks where each variable was *last defined*. When a variable v is used at statement s_{use}, the hash table is looked up using the identifier of v to fetch the statement that last defined it, s_{def}. The occurrence of the def–use (v, s_{def}, s_{use}) is then recorded.

Finally, the following complicating factors are worth mentioning: (1) the definition and the use must occur within the same thread, ie, the tool must be thread-safe; and (2) it is possible to uniquely identify static and instance variables with certainty, but it is not the case for local variables. In Java, for example, the couple (*class name, static attribute name*) uniquely identifies a static variable; the couple (*object reference, attribute name*) uniquely identifies an instance variable. However, to identify a local variable, one might rely on the *method identifier, thread identifier*, and the *variable's byte code index*, but this is not sufficient for two reasons: (1) the same byte code index could be reused for different variables within the same method; and (2) multiple invocations of a given method result in multiple instances of the seemingly same local variables, but in fact they are not the same. Both of these issues are problematic for most profiling tools involving local variables [7]. But it should be noted that for def–use profiling, issue (2) could be circumvented by clearing the hash table from any entries involving local variables that were inserted between method entry and method exit.

5.2 Profiling Logic Elements

When every predicate in a program contains a single clause, logic coverage converges to branch coverage. That is, combinatorial coverage, active clause coverage, clause coverage, and predicate coverage would all be equivalent to branch coverage. This is not an unlikely scenario, since many profiling tools operate at a low language level (eg, Java byte code, MSIL, or binary), in which there is no support for multiple clauses in predicates.

However, in the general case, the profiler needs to track the truth values of all clauses in a given predicate. Using the example presented in Section 4.2, in order to satisfy

```
void recordCoverage(boolean c1, boolean, c2, boolean c3)
{
  if (c1) {
        if (c2) {
                if (c3) {
                        coverage[1]++; // {true, true, true} is covered
                }
```

```
        else
        {
            coverage[4]++; // {true,true,false} is covered
        }
    }
    else {
            if (c3) {
                coverage[3]++; // {true,false,true} is covered
            }
        }
    }
    else {
        if (c2) {
                if (c3) {
                    coverage[2]++; // {false,true,true} is covered
                }
            }
        }
    }
}
```

restricted active clause coverage, clauses ($c1$, $c2$, $c3$) in predicate ($c1$ && $c2$ && $c3$) should take on the following values: {*true, true, true*}, {*false, true, true*}, {*true, false, true*}, and {*true, true, false*}. A profiling tool could verify whether such requirements are satisfied by inserting a call right before the predicate to the profiler function "recordCoverage()," shown.

Here, a nonzero entry in the coverage array indicates that the associated test requirement was satisfied. Given the test requirements, generating functions such as "recordCoverage()" could easily be automated.

6. EFFICIENT PROFILING FOR PATH COVERAGE

If the aim of profiling is to approximate the execution path of a program, then path profiling is obviously most desirable. However, in the presence of loops, the number of potential paths becomes unbounded, making path profiling infeasible. One way to tame this problem is to consider acyclic paths only, ie, when enumerating the paths to be tracked, ignore the cycle causing edges in the CFG, or back-edges. This approach renders profiling more manageable; nevertheless, the number of acyclic paths in a program is still exponential in the number of conditional statements it contains.

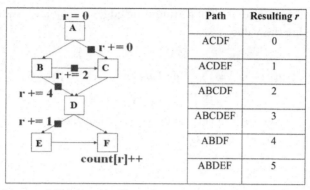

Path	Resulting r
ACDF	0
ACDEF	1
ABCDF	2
ABCDEF	3
ABDF	4
ABDEF	5

Fig. 3 Acyclic control flow graph with probes.

Ball and Larus [14] presented an algorithm for intraprocedural profiling of acyclic paths, which is deemed efficient as its overhead averaged only 31%, while (efficient) branch profiling averaged 16% using the same benchmark. Although the work was published almost two decades ago, we opted to include it in this chapter as it is still considered state of the art due to its innovation, efficiency, and striking simplicity.

To illustrate the algorithm, consider the acyclic CFG in Fig. 3 in which edges labeled by small squares contain probes that increment variable r by some preset value. Note how there are six unique paths from node A to node F and each path results in a different value for r, as shown in the table. When node F is reached, the value of r uniquely identifies the path that was traversed, and thus is used to index into array "int count[5]," which tracks the frequency of execution of each of the six paths. For example, if path ABDF was executed, r takes on the value 4, and count[4] is incremented by 1. Therefore, at the end of execution, count[] fully captures the frequency of occurrence of every path in the CFG. Next, we describe the main steps of the algorithm.

6.1 Assigning Values to Edges

First, a weight or value $Val(e)$ must be assigned to each edge e in the acyclic CFG, such that the sum of values along any path from the entry node to the exit node: (a) is unique; and (b) lies in the range $[0, n-1]$, where n is the number of paths.

The algorithm below computes $Val(e)$ by visiting the nodes of the CFG in reverse topological order, which ensures that all the successors of a node v are visited before v itself. $NumPaths(v)$ is also computed for each node v, which represents the number of paths from v to the exit node. When visiting

v, the algorithm considers all of v's outgoing edges $v \rightarrow w_i$ and assigns the kth outgoing edge the value:

$$Val(v \rightarrow w_k) = \sum_{i=1}^{k-1} NumPaths(w_i), \text{ where } 1 \leq i \leq n$$

```
for each vertex v in reverse topological order {
    if v is a leaf vertex {
1.      NumPaths(v) = 1;
    } else {
        NumPaths(v) = 0;
        for each edge e = v→w {
2.          Val(e) = NumPaths(v);
3.          NumPaths(v) += NumPaths(w);
        }
    }
}
```

To illustrate the algorithm of this step, consider the acyclic CFG in Fig. 4. Note that in case this CFG contained any cycles, the corresponding back-edges would first be removed before proceeding. The nodes are visited in the order FEDCBA (ie, in reverse topological order):

(a) *Visiting F:* Since F is a leaf node, line 1 sets *NumPaths*(F) to 1.

(b) *Visiting E:* Since E is the source of the single edge $E \rightarrow F$, the loop only iterates once yielding $Val(E \rightarrow F) = 0$ due to line 2, and $NumPaths(E) = 0 + NumPaths(F) = 1$ due to line 3.

(c) *Visiting D:* Since D is the source of two edges, the loop iterates twice. The first iteration involves $D \rightarrow F$ yielding $Val(D \rightarrow F) = 0$ and

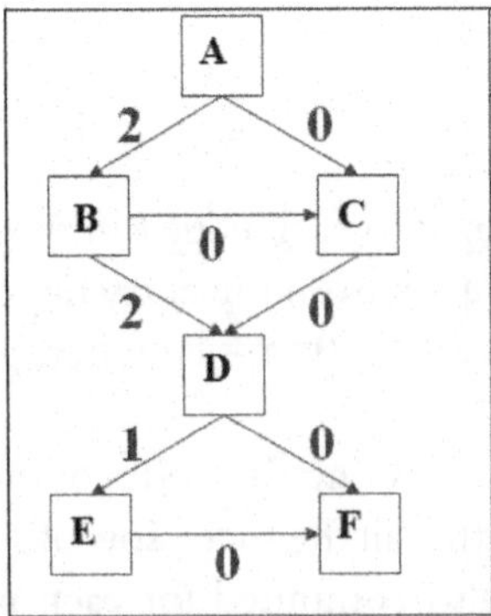

Visited Node	NumPath(v)	Edge Values
F	1	—
E	1	Val(E→F) = 0
D	2	Val(D→F) = 0 Val(D→E) = 1
C	2	Val(C→D) = 0
B	4	Val(B→C) = 0 Val(B→D) = 2
A	6	Val(A→C) = 0 Val(A→B) = 2

Fig. 4 Acyclic control flow graph with edge values.

$NumPaths(D) = 0 + NumPaths(F) = 1$. The second iteration involves $D \rightarrow E$ yielding $Val(D \rightarrow E) = NumPaths(D) = 1$ due to line 2, and $NumPaths(D) = 1 + NumPaths(E) = 2$.

(d) *Visiting C:* The only iteration involves $C \rightarrow D$ yielding $Val(C \rightarrow D) = 0$ and $NumPaths(C) = 0 + NumPaths(D) = 2$.

(e) *Visiting B:* The first iteration involves $B \rightarrow C$ yielding $Val(B \rightarrow C) = 0$ and $NumPaths(B) = 0 + NumPaths(C) = 2$. The second iteration involves $B \rightarrow D$ yielding $Val(B \rightarrow D) = NumPaths(B) = 2$, and $NumPaths(B) = 2 + NumPaths(D) = 4$.

(f) *Visiting A:* The first iteration involves $A \rightarrow C$ yielding $Val(A \rightarrow C) = 0$ and $NumPaths(A) = 0 + NumPaths(C) = 2$. The second iteration involves $A \rightarrow B$ yielding $Val(A \rightarrow B) = NumPaths(A) = 2$, and $NumPaths(A) = 2 + NumPaths(B) = 6$, indicating that six paths are possible in the CFG.

The table in Fig. 4 shows the results of visiting each given node v, ie, $NumPaths(v)$ and zero or more $Val(v \rightarrow w_i)$. In addition, each edge e in the CFG of Fig. 4 is annotated with its corresponding $Val(e)$.

6.2 Selecting Edges for Instrumentation

The proposed path profiling approach could be implemented by inserting probes at every edge in the CFG that will use the values computed in the previous section. However, for efficiency purposes it is desirable to insert probes at a subset of the CFG edges that will likely exhibit a low frequency of execution. These edges and their corresponding weights are identified as follows:

1. A maximum spanning tree of the CFG is computed, where the weight of an edge represents its execution frequency. Since determining such frequencies requires edge profiling which is costly, the authors opted to approximate them statically using a technique they previously presented [15].

2. The chords of the maximum spanning tree are identified, ie, edges in the CFG that are not part of the spanning tree. The probes will be inserted at the chords since their combined execution frequencies will potentially be minimal.

3. The values assigned to the chords must compensate for the values of the edges that were excluded. Given a chord c, its value is computed as follows: (a) an acyclic path from the entry node to the exit node traversing c is identified; (b) in case c is the only chord in that path, it will be assigned

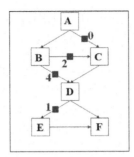

Fig. 5 CFG with probes.

the sum of the values of all the edges in it; (c) in case multiple chords are in the path, the algorithm ensures that the sum of what is to assign to the chords is equal to the sum of the values of all the edges in the path, as detailed in Ref. [15].

Applying the above onto the CFG of Fig. 4 results in the CFG shown in Fig. 5, which shows the probes annotated with their corresponding values. Considering the path ABDF that traverses a single chord $B \rightarrow D$. The value 4 assigned to $B \rightarrow D$ is computed by summing $Val(A \rightarrow B) = 2$, $Val(B \rightarrow D) = 2$, and $Val(D \rightarrow F) = 0$.

6.3 Regenerating a Path from Its Value

Following test suite execution, the frequency of occurrence of every path in the CFG is recorded in count[]. To regenerate a path profile from the counters in count[], it is necessary to relate the integer representing a path to the path itself. This requires the use of the edge values computed in Section 6.1 as below:

1. Let v be a node in the annotated CFG
2. Set v to be the entry node
3. Let r be the path value, ie, count[r] is the frequency of execution of the path to regenerate from r
4. Among the edges outgoing from v, identify edge e having the largest value such that $Val(e) \leq r$
5. Traverse edge e and update v to be the target of e, and r as follows: $r = r - Val(e)$
6. If the exit node is not reached, go to 4

Considering the CFG in Fig. 5 and assuming that r is 3. At the entry node A, since $Val(A \rightarrow B) > Val(A \rightarrow C)$ and $Val(A \rightarrow B) \leq r$, $A \rightarrow B$ is traversed causing r to be updated to 1. At node B, $B \rightarrow C$ is traversed since $Val(B \rightarrow D) > r$.

At node C, C→D is traversed. At node D, $Val(D \rightarrow E) > Val(D \rightarrow F)$ and $Val(D \rightarrow E) \leq r$ so D→E is traversed causing r to be updated to 0. Finally, F is reached via E→F. Therefore, when r is 3, the algorithm generates path ABCDEF, which expectedly is the only path whose cost is 3.

6.4 Dealing with Loops

When identifying the edge values and probe increments, the proposed algorithm ignores the presence of cycle causing back-edges. As a result, the execution of a given back-edge n times would not be recorded as if n additional paths were executed. However, the algorithm will record that the path(s) going through the loop executed n times. To illustrate how this is achieved, consider the cyclical CFG in Fig. 6. In order to handle cycles, each back-edge (E→B in this case) is instrumented with "count[r]++" followed by "r=0" which records the path up to the back-edge (count[r]++) and prepares to record the path after the back-edge (r = 0). This causes a problem though, as different paths might yield the same value of r, as shown in the table of Fig. 6. For example, {ABDEF, ABDE, BDE, BDEF} all have 2 as the value of r. However, paths starting at the entry node and ending at the exit node will have different values of r, ie, ABCEF and ABDEF. To remedy this problem the following steps are taken, which are described in detail in Ref. [15]:

(1) For each node v that is the target of a back-edge, a dummy edge from the entry node to v is added.

(2) For each node w that is the source of a back-edge, a dummy edge from w to the exit node is added.

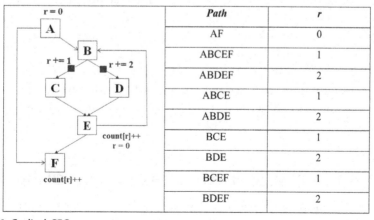

Path	r
AF	0
ABCEF	1
ABDEF	2
ABCE	1
ABDE	2
BCE	1
BDE	2
BCEF	1
BDEF	2

Fig. 6 Cyclical CFG.

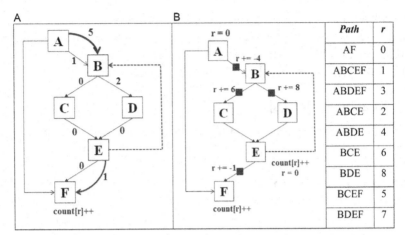

Fig. 7 Transformed CFG, probes, and paths with unique values.

(3) The back-edges are removed.

(4) The edge values and probe increments are computed, as in Sections 6.1 and 6.2.

The basic idea is that the dummy edges create additional paths from the entry node to the exit node that the algorithm in Section 6.1 takes into account. The dummy edge originating from the entry node corresponds to reinitializing the path value along the loop's back-edge. The dummy edge incident on the exit node corresponds to incrementing the path counter along the back-edge. Fig. 7A shows the transformed CFG along with the two added edges, and new edge values. Note how the dummy edges are assigned values, whereas the back-edge is not. Fig. 7B shows the probes' locations and increments and the table in Fig. 7 shows the nine recorded paths along with their path values, which are unique and fall in the $[0, 8]$ range.

To illustrate how the proposed acyclic path profiling can capture the number of loop iterations, consider the execution path $A^1B^1C^1E^1B^2C^2E^2$ $B^3D^1E^3F^1$. At E^1, count[2] is incremented indicating that ABCE executed. At E^2, count[6] is incremented indicating that BCE executed. At E^3, count [8] is incremented indicating that BDE executed. Finally at F^1, count[7] is incremented indicating that BDEF executed.

7. TEST CASE GENERATION FOR PATH COVERAGE

Coverage criteria could be applied on two types of test suites: (1) existing regression test suites that were manually created or collected from the field; and (2) automatically generated test suites. This section is concerned with the latter type. Specifically, since path coverage is the ultimate form of structural coverage (in the sense that it subsumes all other structural coverage techniques), the focus here will be on test case generation techniques that inherently aim at increasing path coverage. Noting that other strategies have also been shown to be successful, such as those categorized as evolutionary [16] or random based.

This section reviews *symbolic execution*, in its both static and dynamic contexts, since it is at the heart of test case generation approaches that aim at increasing path coverage.

7.1 Static Symbolic Execution

Static symbolic execution [17], or simply *symbolic execution*, is a technique that aims at computing all possible paths in a program and representing each symbolically. One form of symbolic path representation is a *path condition* (PC). A PC is a first-order formula (FOL) such that the inputs satisfying it execute the associated path. Theoretically, the technique is capable of generating the set of test cases that induces all possible paths in a program without requiring its execution by finding one satisfying input for each PC. Fig. 8 illustrates how symbolic execution works. This code has three potential paths represented by execution traces $p_1 = \langle l_1, l_2, l_8 \rangle$, $p_2 = \langle l_1, l_2, l_3, l_4, l_5, l_6, l_8 \rangle$, and $p_3 = \langle l_1, l_2, l_3, l_4, l_5, l_6, l_7, l_8 \rangle$. The goal of symbolic execution is to provide for each of the three paths a test case that induces it, ie, a test case t_1 that induces p_1, t_2 that induces p_2, and t_3 that induces p_3.

This is typically achieved via emulating abstract program execution while traversing the binary computation tree of the program in a depth-first manner [17,18]. In a computation tree, each inner node represents the

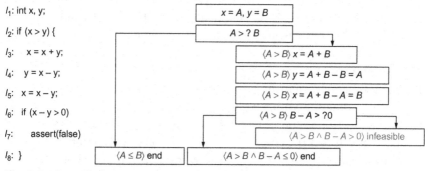

l_1: int x, y;		$x = A, y = B$
l_2: if (x > y) {		$A > ? B$
l_3: x = x + y;		$\langle A > B \rangle\, x = A + B$
l_4: y = x − y;		$\langle A > B \rangle\, y = A + B − B = A$
l_5: x = x − y;		$\langle A > B \rangle\, x = A + B − A = B$
l_6: if (x − y > 0)		$\langle A > B \rangle\, B − A > ?0$
l_7: assert(false)		$\langle A > B \land B − A > 0 \rangle$ infeasible
l_8: }	$\langle A \leq B \rangle$ end	$\langle A > B \land B − A \leq 0 \rangle$ end

Fig. 8 Static symbolic execution at work.

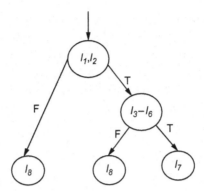

Fig. 9 Computation tree.

execution of a conditional statement, and each edge represents the execution of a sequence of nonconditional statements. For each path p in the tree, symbolic execution constructs a PC that characterizes the input assignments for which the program executes along p. A path condition is an FOL over constraints on input values. If a path condition is satisfiable, then the corresponding path is feasible. Fig. 9 shows the computation tree corresponding to the code in Fig. 8.

The steps for generating t_1, t_2, and t_3 are as follows:

1. The abstract execution keeps a symbolic value for each variable in the program and also keeps path conditions that must be satisfied for the execution to proceed.

2. The symbolic execution starts with the variables "x" and "y" assuming the symbolic values of "A" and "B," respectively.

3. Two branches are possible at the "if" condition of line l_2. The *false* branch results in $p_1 = \langle l_1, l_2, l_8 \rangle$ with an associated path condition of "$A \leq B$." Symbolic execution typically uses a propositional logic satisfiability (SAT) solver or an FOL satisfiability modulo theory (SMT–SAT) solver to find a satisfying assignment (values for "A" and "B") for "$A \leq B$," yielding test case $t_1(x = A = 0, y = B = 1)$ as one possibility.

4. The *true* branch originating from line l_2 goes to line l_3 inside the body of the "if" condition with a path condition of "$A > B$."

5. The symbolic execution updates the values of "x" and "y" with each statement. It uses the constraint solver to resolve and simplify the values and the path conditions. For example, this enables simplifying the path condition expression "$A + B - B$" to "A" on line l_4.

6. The *false* branch originating from line l_6 results in $p_2 = \langle l_1, l_2, l_3, l_4, l_5, l_6,$ $l_8 \rangle$ with an associated path condition of "$(A > B) \wedge (B - A \leq 0)$," yielding test case $t_2(x = 1, y = 0)$ as one possibility.

7. Since the path condition "$(A > B) \wedge (B - A > 0)$" which is associated with $p_3 = \langle l_1, l_2, l_3, l_4, l_5, l_6, l_7, l_8 \rangle$ could never be satisfied, the SMT solver would determine that p_3 is infeasible.

In the presence of unbounded loops, both static and dynamic symbolic executions suffer from the *path explosion* problem, which translates into unmanageably deep computation trees. This problem is typically addressed by bounding the depths of the trees, which will obviously impact the effectiveness of the approach. In addition, static symbolic execution is especially limited by the power of the underlying constraint solver. Consider the following example presented in Ref. [19]:

```
int obscure(int x, int y) {
    if (x == hash(y)) return -1; // error
    return 0; // ok
}
```

If properly designed, the "hash()" function should not return a value that straightforwardly conveys any information about its input; ie, the relationship between its input and output should be complex. In such a case, existing constraint solvers would not be capable of generating inputs (values for x and y) that satisfy the condition "x == hash(y)," thus rendering static symbolic execution ineffective. This problem is rather common, as it is also manifested when pointers and nonlinear arithmetic expressions are involved. Pointers are a complicating factor since they require corresponding objects to be present and aliases to be inferred. Nonlinear expressions are problematic since existing solvers can only handle sets of linear equations. In order to address this shortcoming, Korel [20,21] proposed *dynamic symbolic execution*.

7.2 Dynamic Symbolic Execution

Test case generation via *dynamic symbolic execution*, or DSE, typically proceeds as follows [18,22,23]:

1. Similar to static symbolic execution, the goal is to traverse the binary computation tree of the subject program in a depth-first manner.

2. The program is concretely executed with some given or random input t_1 that induces path p_1 in the tree.

3. Concurrently, the program is symbolically executed and path constraints on inputs are gathered at conditional statements along p_1.

4. The gathered constraints are altered by negating the constraint associated with the deepest conditional statement in p_1 that has not been negated before. An SMT solver is applied onto the resulting constraints in order to generate input t_2 that is meant to induce path p_2 that would be most similar to p_1 among the paths that have not been traversed before.

5. The program is concretely executed with t_2, and steps 3 and 4 are performed on t_2 resulting in t_3 and so on until the computation tree is fully traversed.

Dynamic symbolic execution is no different from its static counterpart in that it aims at generating a test case for each path in the computation tree. However, DSE benefits from executing the program both concretely and symbolically as follows:

1. When the symbolic expressions fall into nondecidable theories such as when they contain nonlinear subexpressions, the SMT–SAT solvers return inconclusive results. DSE then replaces the expression by its associated concrete value.

2. Pointers in constraints are handled either by including a memory model or by replacing them by their corresponding concrete values. This is done to avoid pointer arithmetic and the inclusion of complex memory modeling and is justified by looking for NULL pointer defects solely.

3. On the other hand, symbolic execution helps generate concrete inputs for the next similar execution, thus resulting in better path coverage.

Several research and industry tools support the DSE technique. DART [23] derives a model of the program interface, generates a directed random test suite based on the model, and then refines the generated test suite by adding randomly generated test cases that increase path coverage systematically. DART targets standard errors such as crashes and nontermination assertion violations.

CUTE [18] presents a concolic (concrete-symbolic) execution technique that starts with executing the program on a randomly generated input. CUTE records the path conditions of the paths executed by the input. It systematically flips predicates in the collected path conditions that lead to paths that have not been explored before. It queries the SMT solver for satisfying assignment to the modified path conditions. It uses the returned satisfying assignments as test cases that increase path coverage.

SAGE [22], PEX [24], and YOGI [25] from Microsoft research follow the same suit of DART. SAGE is a variant of DART that uses fuzzing in order to detect security defects. PEX targets .NET binaries and generates parametrized-unit tests for .NET programs. YOGI additionally checks the feasibility of program paths using a counterexample refinement methodology similar to SLAM [26].

KLEE [27] extends the concept of symbolic execution with constraint solving optimizations and with search heuristics that enable increasing code coverage metrics. The optimizations and the heuristics enable KLEE to work on real size applications.

8. TEST SUITE MINIMIZATION: COVERING COMPLEX *TR*'S

Given a program P, a test suite T, and a set of test requirements TR that are covered by T. *Test suite minimization* (also referred to as *test suite reduction* in the literature) aims at finding T', a minimal subset of T, that covers all test requirements in TR. The conjecture is that (the smaller) T' would be as effective as T in revealing defects.

The authors in Ref. [5] conducted an empirical study to assess the impact of using complex test requirements as opposed to basic test requirements in test suite minimization, with respect to its effectiveness at revealing defects. The complex program elements they considered were *slice pairs* and *information flow pairs*. This section presents the part of the work presented in Ref. [5] that relates to coverage-based test suite minimization.

8.1 Coverage-Based Test Suite Minimization

The main reasons for minimizing test suites are: (1) to reduce the cost of test suite execution and (2) to reduce the number of test executions for which it is necessary either to manually determine correct output or to audit (manually check) actual output. Typically, the cost of manually determining or auditing output dominates the cost of test suite execution. Coverage-based *test suite minimization* selects test cases from T to include in T' in a way that maximizes the proportion of program elements that are covered. It attempts to cover as many of the elements covered by T with as few test cases as possible. A coverage-maximizing subset of a test suite is an instance of the *set-cover problem*, which is NP-complete but which admits a greedy approximation algorithm [28]. On each of its iterations, the greedy algorithm selects the test that covers the largest number of elements not covered by the previously selected tests. This specific approach was termed *basic coverage maximization* in Ref. [5].

8.2 Covering Complex Program Elements

In coverage-based test suite minimization, the profiles used to characterize test executions indicate the execution frequency of certain program elements that are believed to be relevant to whether executions succeed or fail. Profiling reduces a complete execution history to a more compact form that is amenable to analysis. For a failed execution to be revealed, its profile must differ in some way from the profiles of successful executions. One of the main goals of the work described in Ref. [5] is to measure the effect of varying the type of the covered program elements on the effectiveness of coverage-based test suite minimization. The authors employed several types of profiles with program elements of different complexities:

- Method calls (*MC*) or functions: For every method *M* that is executed in at least one test, an *MC* profile contains a count of how many times *M* is called in the current test.

- Method call pairs (*MCP*) or function pairs: For every combination of methods *M1* and *M2* such that *M1* calls *M2* in at least one test, an *MCP* profile contains a count of how many times *M1* calls *M2* in the current test.

- Basic blocks (*BB*): For every basic block *B* such that *B* is executed in at least one test, a *BB* profile contains a count of how many times *B* is executed in the current test.

- Basic block edges (*BBE*) or branches: For every pair of basic blocks *B1* and *B2* such that there is a branch from *B1* to *B2* in at least one test, a *BBE* profile contains a count of how many times this branch is taken in the current test.

- Def-use pairs (*DUP*): For every pair consisting of a variable definition $D(x)$ and a use $U(x)$ such that $D(x)$ dynamically reaches $U(x)$ in at least one test, a *DUP* profile contains a count of how many times $D(x)$ dynamically reaches $U(x)$ in the current test.

- All simpler profiles combined (*ALL*): Combined counts of *MC*, *MCP*, *BB*, *BBE*, and *DUP*.

- Information flow pairs (*IFP*): For each combination of variables x and y such that information flowed dynamically from x into y in at least one test, an *IFP* profile contains a count of how many times such a flow occurred in the current test.

- Slice pairs (*SliceP*): For each pair of statements s_1 and s_2 such that s_1 occurs in a (backward) dynamic slice [29,30] on s_2 in at least one test, a *SliceP* profile contains a count of how many times s_1 occurs in such a slice.

IFP and *SliceP* are clearly the most complex among the above eight program elements. *IFP* is based on *dynamic information flow analysis*, and *SliceP* is based on *dynamic slicing*, both of which are described in detail in Ref. [7]. Here, we describe them briefly with the help of the Java code below:

```
s1: x = 1;
s2: y = 1;
s3: b = -1;
s4: if (b >0) {
s5:    z = x;
       } else {
s6:    z = y;
       }
```

Informally, in the context of static analysis, a statement t is *directly control dependent* on a statement s, denoted t *DCD* s, if the control structure of the program indicates that s decides, via the branches it controls, whether t is executed or not, eg, s_5 *DCD* s_4 and s_6 *DCD* s_4. The dynamic counterpart of the *DCD* relation is the *dynamic direct control dependence* relation or *DDynCD*. An *action* s^k is an executing program statement where s is the statement and k is the position in the execution trace. For example, the code above induces the following execution trace $\langle s_1^1, s_2^2, s_3^3, s_4^4, s_6^5 \rangle$ in which action s_6^5 indicates that statement s_6 was the fifth statement to execute in the trace. Action t^m is *directly dynamically control dependent* on action s^k, denoted t^m *DDynCD* s^k, if s^k is the most recent predicate action to occur prior to action t^m such that t *DCD* s, eg, s_6^5 *DDynCD* s_4^4.

Informally, action t^m is *directly dynamically data dependent* on action s^k, denoted t^m *DDynDD* s^k, if and only if t^m uses a variable or an object that was last defined by s^k, eg, s_6^5 *DDynDD* s_2^2. The *DDynDD* relation models both intraprocedural and interprocedural data dependences. The latter occur when an execution trace spans different functions and the data defined in one function are used in another.

In addition to the *DDynCD* and *DDynDD* relations, three other kinds of dynamic dependences between actions could be identified, each of which is interprocedural:

(1) Use of a value returned by a return statement

(2) Use of a value passed by a formal parameter

(3) Control dependence on a calling method's invoke instruction

The combination of the aforementioned five types of dependences comprises what is called "direct influence." Given two actions s^k and t^m with $k < m$, s^k *directly influences* t^m, denoted s^k *DInfluence* t^m, if and only if t^m exhibits any of these five types of dependences upon s^k. The set of actions that t^m is directly influenced by is denoted $DInfluence(t^m)$, eg, $DInfluence(s_6^5) = \{s_4^4, s_2^2\}$.

The dynamic information flow analysis adopted to compute the $IFPs$ is based on the following inductive equation:

$$InfoFlow(t^m) = U(t^m) \cup \bigcup_{s^k \in DInfluence(t^m)} InfoFlow(s^k)$$

Here $U(t^m)$ is the set of objects used at t^m and $DInfluence(t^m)$ is the set of actions that directly influence t^m. $InfoFlow(t^m)$, the set of objects that flow into (or influence) t^m, comprises the objects used at t^m and all the objects from which information flows into the actions that directly influence t^m. For example, $InfoFlow(s_6^5) = \{y, b\}$ which yields two information flow pairs (s_2, y, s_6, z) and (s_3, b, s_6, z). The first quadruple states that information flowed from y (last defined at s_2) to z (last defined at s_6).

The dynamic slicing algorithm is based on the following inductive equation:

$$DynSlice(t^m) = \{t\} \cup \bigcup_{s^k \in DInfluence(t^m)} DynSlice(s^k)$$

$DynSlice(t^m)$, the set of statements that influence t^m, comprises the statement t itself and all the statements that influence the actions that directly influence t^m. For example, $DynSlice(s_6^5) = \{s_6, s_4, s_3, s_2\}$ which yields three slice pairs (s_4, s_6), (s_3, s_6), and (s_2, s_6).

8.3 Motivating Example

Coverage-based test suite minimization conjectures that for a failed execution to be revealed, its profile must differ in some way from the profiles of successful executions. This section presents an example in which such conjecture does not apply when basic program elements are used, but does apply when IFP profiles are used.

Consider the Java method shown in Table 1 where statement 5 is faulty; the + operator should have been a −. Note how both the faulty and correct statements assign the same value to y except when x[i] is equal to −1. Therefore, the failure is triggered only in the case when one or more elements of x[] are equal to −1. Table 1 also shows the following: (a) test suite $T = \{t1, t2, t3, t4, t5, t6\}$ in which each test case comprises three elements of x[], two of the test cases trigger a failure and the other four do not; and (b) the statement coverage information for each test case: a check mark

Table 1 Java Code and Statement Coverage Information for the Motivating Example

/* Statement 5 is faulty. The correct statement is: y = -x[i] - 1/x[i]; */ public static void foo(int [] x) {	Passing Test Cases			Failing Test Cases		
	t1(1,2,3)	t2(0,1,2)	t3(2,3,4)	t4(5,300,1)	t5(3,1,100)	t6(100,1,1)
1 int y; int z;	✓	✓	✓	✓	✓	✓
2 for (int i = 0; i < x.length; i++){	✓	✓	✓	✓	✓	✓
3 y = 0;	✓	✓	✓	✓	✓	✓
4 if (x[i] < 0) {	✓	✓	✓	✓	✓	✓
5 y = -x[i] + 1/x[i];	✓	✓	✓	✓	✓	✓
6 } else if (x[i] > 0) {	✓	✓		✓		✓
7 y = x[i] - 1/x[i];	✓	✓		✓		✓
}						
8 if (y == 0) {	✓	✓	✓	✓	✓	✓
9 z = ...	✓	✓		✓	✓	✓
} else {						
10 z = ...	✓	✓	✓	✓	✓	✓
} } 11 }						

Table 2 Branch Coverage Information for the Motivating Example

Branch (Source Statement, Target Statement)	Passing Test Cases				Failing Test Cases	
	t1(1, 2, −3)	t2(0, 1, −2)	t3(−2, −3, −4)	t4(−5, −300, 1)	t5(−3, −1, −100)	t6(100, 1, −1)
(8,9)	✓	✓		✓	✓	✓
(2,3)	✓	✓	✓	✓	✓	✓
(4,5)	✓	✓	✓	✓	✓	✓
(2,11)	✓	✓	✓	✓	✓	✓
(8,10)	✓	✓	✓	✓	✓	✓
(6,7)	✓	✓		✓		✓
(4,6)	✓	✓		✓		✓

Table 3 Def-Use Coverage Information for the Motivating Example

Def-Use (Def Statement, Use Statement)	Passing Test Cases				Failing Test Cases	
	t1(1, 2, −3)	t2(0, 1, −2)	t3(−2, −3, −4)	t4(−5, −300, 1)	t5(−3, −1, −100)	t6(100, 1, −1)
(y,5,8)	✓	✓	✓	✓	✓	✓
(y,7,8)	✓	✓		✓		✓

indicates that the statement at the given row was executed at least once using the test case at the given column. Similarly, Table 2 shows the branch coverage information for T, and Table 3 shows the corresponding def-use coverage information.

Applying coverage-based test suite minimization on each of the set of the profiles shown in Tables 1–3 could possibly yield a reduced test suite $T' = \{t1\}$, since in all three cases, $t1$ covers all the elements covered by T. However, even though T' is minimal in size, it does not include any failing test cases, and thus is not effective at revealing the fault.

Table 4 shows the IFP coverage information. Note how $IFP(5,y,9,z)$ is only covered by both failing test cases $t5$ and $t6$. Which dictates that the minimized test suite T' must include at least one of them. Therefore, in this case T' will be effective at revealing the fault (although it must contain at least two tests).

Table 4 Information Flow Coverage Information for the Motivating Example

IFP (Source Statement, Source Object, Target Statement, Target Object)	Passing Test Cases				Failing Test Cases	
	t1(1, 2, −3)	t2(0, 1, −2)	t3(−2, −3, −4)	t4(−5, −300, 1)	t5(−3, −1, −100)	t6(100, 1, −1)
(5,y,9,z)					✓	✓
(6,-,10,z)	✓					✓
(7,y,10,z)	✓					✓
(8,-,9,z)	✓	✓		✓	✓	✓
(2,-,9,z)	✓	✓		✓	✓	✓
(4,-,9,z)	✓	✓		✓	✓	✓
(5,y,8,-)	✓	✓	✓	✓	✓	✓
(2,-,4,-)	✓	✓	✓	✓	✓	✓
(2,-,8,-)	✓	✓	✓	✓	✓	✓
(2,-,3,y)	✓	✓	✓	✓	✓	✓
(4,-,5,y)	✓	✓	✓	✓	✓	✓
(8,-,10,z)	✓	✓	✓	✓	✓	✓
(2,-,5,y)	✓	✓	✓	✓	✓	✓
(2,-,10,z)	✓	✓	✓	✓	✓	✓
(4,-,8,-)	✓	✓	✓	✓	✓	✓
(4,-,10,z)	✓	✓	✓	✓	✓	✓
(7,y,8,-)	✓	✓		✓		✓
(6,-,7,y)	✓	✓		✓		✓
(4,-,6,-)	✓	✓		✓		✓
(4,-,7,y)	✓	✓		✓		✓
(2,-,6,-)	✓	✓		✓		✓
(7,y,9,z)	✓	✓		✓		✓
(6,-,8,-)	✓	✓		✓		✓
(2,-,7,y)	✓	✓		✓		✓
(6,-,9,z)	✓	✓		✓		✓
(5,y,10,z)	✓	✓	✓	✓	✓	
...	.	..				

Note that in case the source and the target are conditional statements a "-" is used in place of the object name.

8.4 Empirical Study

Coverage-based test suite minimization, and specifically basic coverage maximization, was applied to data sets derived from three subject programs. It was used with each of the eight profile types described in Section 8.2, thus yielding eight different variations. Simple random sampling was employed as a baseline technique.

8.4.1 Experimental Setup

The variations considered were compared principally with respect to the average percentage of defects that they revealed over a number of replicated applications, viewed as a function of the number of tests selected. The number of tests selected for a given program is dictated by varying the type of profiles used.

Basic coverage maximization was accomplished for each subject program and profile type by applying the greedy selection algorithm described in Section 8.1 to the profiles of that type that were collected for the subject program. A program element was considered to be covered by a test if its corresponding profile entry was nonzero. For example, a test was considered to cover a particular information flow pair if the corresponding element of the test's *IFP* profile was nonzero. Note that the greedy algorithm sometimes encounters ties (different tests that each covers the maximal number of program elements not covered by previously selected tests). The way ties are broken affects the number of tests selected. To address this in the experiments, basic coverage maximization was replicated 1000 times for each program/profile-type combination, first randomly permuting the order of the tests. For each replication the authors recorded how many tests were selected and how many failures and defects were found and then they used their respective averages in their analysis.

The performance statistics for simple random sampling (baseline technique) were computed by randomly selecting tests (without replacement) from the given test suite and recording the number of failure-inducing tests that were selected and the number of defects revealed. To account for the variability of the samples, this procedure was replicated 1000 times and the results were averaged.

In some cases, the raw profiles that were collected in the study contained a large amount of redundant information [31]. For example, there were groups of basic blocks that were always executed together, and therefore their counts were the same in each execution. This redundant information was removed by replacing each group of profiles features that always had the same value (count) by a single feature. For example, when one subject program (*JTidy*) was tested, close to 2.9 million distinct slice pairs were detected. These were replaced by 331,004 unique features.

8.4.2 Subject Programs and Test Suites

In the experiments three Java programs were used: the *javac* Java compiler version 1.3.1 (28,639 lines of code), the *Xerces* XML parser version 2.1 (52,528 lines of code), and the *JTidy* HTML syntax checker and pretty printer version 3 (9153 lines of code).

javac was tested with the *Jacks* test suite, which tests compliance with the Java Language Specification. The Jacks test suite comprises 3140 tests (each containing six lines of code on average) among which 233 caused *javac* to fail.

Xerces was tested by using part of the XML Conformance Test Suite (XML TS), which provides a set of metrics for determining conformance to the W3C XML Recommendation. There are 2000 tests in the XML TS contributed by several organizations such as Sun Microsystems and IBM. Only 1667 tests were used in the experiments (each containing 15 lines of code on average) resulting in 10 failures. Note that 333 tests were excluded because it was difficult to determine with certainty whether those tests passed or failed. *Xerces* was configured to check only the syntax and not the semantics of the input XML files, ie, to simply check whether the files were well formed.

JTidy was tested using 1000 files (each containing 280 lines on average) downloaded from the Google Groups (groups.google.com) using a web crawler. Of these, five were XML files and the rest were HTML files. *JTidy* failed on 47 of these test cases.

The defects causing the failures were investigated manually and the failures were classified into groups believed to have been caused by the same defect. For *javac*, 67 distinct defects were believed to have caused the 233 failures. For *Xerces*, 5 distinct defects were believed to have caused the 10 failures. For *JTidy*, 8 defects were believed to have caused the 47 failures.

8.4.3 Profile Characteristics

Table 5 shows for each program and profile type the number of unique profile features (unique counts) and the number of original profile features (original counts) that were generated while running the test suites. For example, in the *SliceP* profiles for *Xerces*, there were 84,565 unique profile

Table 5 Number of Unique and Original Counts (Profile Features) Encountered During Execution for the Various Types of Profiles

		MC	MCP	BB	BBE	DUP	ALL	IFP	SliceP
Xerces	Unique	361	690	1725	1982	3812	4520	29,712	84,565
	Original	797	1540	6967	7987	24,756	42,047	169,556	2,104,494
JTidy	Unique	208	461	1436	1751	3991	4721	38,405	331,004
	Original	327	723	4912	5714	19,660	31,336	89,871	2,874,715
Javac	Unique	1022	2123	3655	4307	9620	11,315	66,829	762,798
	Original	1281	4066	11,354	13,028	48,127	77,856	270,421	7,884,335

features, each corresponding to a pair of statements s_1 and s_2, such that at least one dynamic slice computed at s_2 contained s_1. The column titled *ALL* shows the combined counts of *MC, MCP, BB, BBE,* and *DUP.* Note how the sum of the original counts for *MC, MCP, BB, BBE,* and *DUP* equals the original count for *ALL,* but as a result of the removal of redundant information, the sum of the unique counts for *MC, MCP, BB, BBE,* and *DUP* exceeds the unique count for *ALL.* As expected, Table 5 shows that more detailed profile types have higher execution counts.

8.4.4 Basic Coverage Maximization Results

The results of performing basic coverage maximization with each of the eight profile types are shown in Table 6. (The columns showing the number of selected tests, revealed failures, and revealed defects represent the outcome of averaging the results of 1000 replications, which explains why they contain fractions.) For example, in the case of *Xerces/IFP,* the greedy coverage maximization algorithm selected a set of tests that comprised, on average, just 10.43% of the original test suite, yet the selected tests covered all of the information flows the original ones did. On average, the selected tests revealed 35.14% of the failures and 70.28% of the defects revealed by the original test suite. It should be noted that both the percentage of defects revealed and the percentage of tests selected need to be considered when comparing the performance of one profile type to that of another. For example, with *Xerces* only 0.84% of the tests were needed, on average, to maximize *MC* coverage. However, no defects were actually revealed, which is clearly not acceptable. With *javac,* on the other hand, maximizing *SliceP* coverage revealed 91.04% of the defects but required 45.19% of the tests to be selected, on average.

In Figs. 10–12, the forms of basic coverage maximization corresponding to each of the profile types are compared to simple random sampling with respect to each technique's average effectiveness for revealing defects.

Fig. 10 shows that with *Xerces* basic coverage maximization performed considerably better than simple random sampling, except with *MC* profiling, which revealed no defects. It also shows that with *Xerces,* maximizing *SliceP* coverage revealed all defects, yet maximizing *IFP* coverage revealed 70.28% of the defects with only half as many tests.

Fig. 11 shows that with *JTidy* basic coverage maximization performed better than simple random sampling for each profile type. Maximizing *SliceP* coverage revealed all the defects but required the selection of 26.73% of the tests. Maximizing *ALL* coverage revealed 94.8% of the defects with only

Table 6 Results for Basic Coverage Maximization

	Profile Type	# Tests Selected	% Tests Selected	# Failures Selected	% Failures Selected	# Defects Revealed	% Defects Revealed
Xerces	*MC*	14	0.84	0	0	0	0
1667 tests	*MCP*	59.53	3.57	1.21	12.11	1.21	24.22
	BB	163.03	9.78	2	20	2	40
	BBE	195.56	11.73	2.34	23.49	2.34	46.98
	DUP	265.75	15.94	4.48	44.86	3	60
0.6% failures	*ALL*	278.73	16.72	4.50	45.03	3	60
	IFP	174	10.43	3.51	35.14	3.51	70.28
	SliceP	344.05	20.63	7	70	5	**100**
JTidy	*MC*	10	1	2	4.25	2	25
1000 tests	*MCP*	30.48	3.05	5.56	11.84	4.50	56.27
	BB	51.28	5.12	10.15	21.60	4.51	56.45
	BBE	64.5	6.45	13.31	28.33	6.49	81.2
	DUP	119.86	11.98	19.22	40.90	6.62	82.82
4.7% failures	*ALL*	123.63	12.36	20.19	42.97	7.58	94.8
	IFP	128.43	12.84	20.92	44.51	7	87.5
	SliceP	267.33	26.73	30	63.82	8	**100**
Javac	*MC*	51.41	1.63	9.19	3.94	9.19	13.72
3140 tests	*MCP*	164.34	5.23	15.15	6.502	15.14	22.60
	BB	245.07	7.80	20.07	8.613	19.1	28.50
	BBE	315.76	10.05	25.22	10.82	21.92	32.72
	DUP	572.13	18.22	53.01	22.75	41.91	62.55
7.42% failures	*ALL*	606.31	19.30	55.14	23.66	42.39	63.27
	IFP	589.59	18.77	57.51	24.68	45.62	68.10
	SliceP	1419	45.19	108	46.35	61	**91.04**

The bold values highlight the best results achieved.

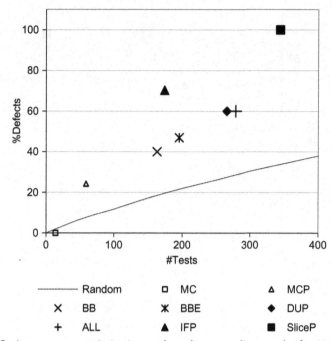

Fig. 10 Basic coverage maximization and random sampling results for *Xerces* (1667 tests, 10 failures, and 5 defects).

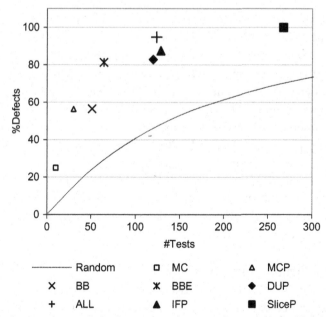

Fig. 11 Basic coverage maximization and random sampling results for *JTidy* (1000 tests, 47 failures, and 8 defects).

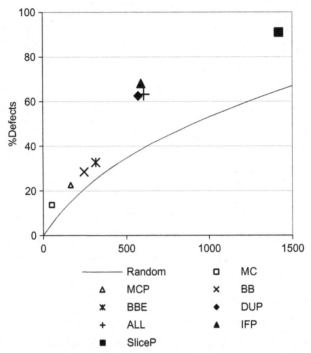

Fig. 12 Basic coverage maximization and random sampling results for *javac* (3140 tests, 233 failures, and 67 defects).

12.36% of the tests. The performance of coverage maximization was very similar with *ALL*, *DUP*, and *IFP* profiles.

Fig. 12 shows that with *javac* coverage maximization revealed defects more effectively than simple random sampling did for all profile types. Also, the more detailed the profiles, the more tests were required to maximize coverage and the more defects were revealed. A significant jump in effectiveness was observed when def-use pairs, information flow pairs, and (especially) slice pairs were covered, although large numbers of tests were required to maximize coverage of these elements.

It is noteworthy that with all of the data sets, maximizing *DUP* coverage performed similar to maximizing *ALL* coverage. This outcome may be related to the fact that all-uses coverage subsumes statement and branch coverage as shown in Section 4.1.

8.4.5 Observations and Cost Analysis

The approach involves the collection and analysis of execution profiles. In most cases the cost of collecting profiles dominated the cost of analyzing

Table 7 Observed Average Execution Times for the Instrumented Subject Programs (The Average Execution Time for Each of the Original Programs was ~1 s.)

	MC/MCP[a] (s)	MC/MCP/BB/BBE[a] (s)	MC/MCP/BB/BBE/DUP[a] (s)	IFP (s)	SliceP (s)
Xerces ~1	2	4		23	29
JTidy ~1	5	90		900	1200
Javac 2	11	114		216	360

[a]The program was instrumented to generate profiles for multiple profile types.

Table 8 Average Execution Profile Sizes

	MC/MCP[a] (kB)	MC/MCP/BB/BBE[a] (kB)	MC/MCP/BB/BBE/DUP[a] (kB)	IFP (kB)	SliceP (kB)
Xerces 30	200	350		400	3000
JTidy 20	250	644		1200	32,000
Javac 25	300	600		2700	20,000

[a]The profiles include information about multiple profile types.

Table 9 Times for Individual Parts of Xerces Analysis, for Different Profile Types

Xerces	MC/MCP/BB/BBE/DUP[a] (s)	IFP (s)	SliceP (s)
Profile consolidation	285	850	5620
Coverage maximization	~1	~2	~10

[a]Reported times are for the combined profile types.

them. Table 7 shows the average execution times of the instrumented subject programs, Table 8 shows the average sizes of the collected profiles, and Table 9 shows the analysis times for Xerces, broken down by the profile type.

As expected, Tables 7 and 8 clearly indicate that time and space requirements increase as the level of profile detail increases. Table 9 indicates that the most time-consuming part of the analysis is profile consolidation, ie, the process of merging information from all the execution profiles. Also, contrasting Tables 7 and 8 makes it clear that the time needed for profile collection was much greater than the time needed for analysis. For example, the time needed to collect the SliceP profiles for Xerces was $29 \times 1667 = 48,384$ s, whereas the time to analyze them was only 5630 s. It should be noted that the times for IFP and SliceP collection are expected to decrease substantially if optimized information flow analysis and slicing algorithms are used [6,30].

In summary, the empirical study showed that: (1) coverage maximization revealed defects more effectively than simple random sampling; (2) coverage maximization based on complex profiles such as *IFP* and *SliceP* profiles revealed defects not revealed with simpler profiles, at the cost of additional tests; and (3) coverage maximization based on *SliceP* profiles revealed the most defects. Hence, the additional cost of using profiles of finer granularity appears justified.

 ## 9. TEST SUITE MINIMIZATION: COVERING COMBINATIONS OF BASIC *TR'S*

The empirical study in Section 8 showed that covering program elements with finer granularity revealed relatively more defects but resulted in larger subsets and higher cost. The authors in Ref. [32] explored test suite minimization by covering combinations of basic program elements of different types. The conjecture is that these combinations are more likely to characterize complex failures and are cheaper to collect since they are based on basic elements. Clearly, exploring all possible combinations induced by a test suite is infeasible, which necessitates the use of an approximation algorithm. Hence, they investigated the use of a genetic algorithm to select a number of suitable combinations of program elements to be covered during minimization.

9.1 Test Suite Minimization

Given a test suite T, the aim is to find the smallest subset T' of T that is capable of revealing most, and preferably all, of the defects revealed by T. The proposed technique is motivated by the following conjectures:

(1) Combinations of program elements are more likely to characterize complex failures [33]. Therefore, a technique based on covering combinations of elements (eg, statements, branches, def-use pairs, etc.) is likely to be more effective than one that covers single types of elements.

(2) The percentage of failing tests is typically much smaller than that of the passing tests. Specifically, each defect typically only causes a small percentage of tests to fail. Therefore, smaller groups of similar tests are more likely to be failure inducing than larger ones.

The main steps of the minimization technique are as follows:

(1) Given a test suite T, generate execution profiles of basic program elements, namely, statements, branches, and def-use pairs.

(2) Choose a threshold M_{fail} for the maximum number of tests that could fail due to a single defect (eg, if $|T| = 1000$, a sensible value of M_{fail} would be 100).

(3) Generate C, a pool of combinations of basic program elements (see Section 9.3).

(4) Extract C' from C, the set of combinations that were covered by less than M_{fail} tests. When possible, the distribution of C' should span the full range $[1, M_{fail}]$. For example, it is desirable that C' includes combinations that occurred in 1 test, 2 tests, 3 tests, ..., M_{fail} tests. Failing to assure that might reduce the effectiveness of the proposed technique as some suspicious combinations might not get included in C'.

(5) Use a greedy algorithm to identify T', the smallest subset of T that covers all the combinations in C'. On each of its iterations, the algorithm selects the test that covers the largest number of combinations not covered by the previously selected tests (more details could be found in Ref. [5]).

Steps (3) and (4) are clearly the most challenging as they entail exploring combinations of program elements whose number is exponential with respect to the number of the basic program elements. Since a brute-force approach is clearly not viable, the authors chose to use a genetic algorithm as an alternative approximation approach, as described next.

9.2 Genetic Algorithm

The aim here is to use a genetic algorithm to generate a number of combinations of basic program elements that are exercised by the least number of tests in T, based on the assumption that such combinations are more likely to be failure inducing than others. In general, a genetic algorithm solves a given problem by operating on an initial population of candidate solutions or *chromosomes*, evaluating their quality using a *fitness function*, applying a form of *transformation* to form new generations and improve the quality of these solutions, and ultimately evolving to a single *solution* or set of solutions that fit certain criteria. The main actors and phases of the algorithm are described below.

9.2.1 Chromosome Representation

In this implementation, a chromosome has to represent a combination of executed statements, branches, and def–use pairs, so a bit string notation can indicate which profiled elements are included in each combination instance. The size of each bit string is equal to the total number of execution elements gathered during profiling; a bit set to **1** implies that the corresponding element is included in this combination, and the number of **1**s in the bit string corresponds to the size of the combination.

9.2.2 Fitness Function

Once a chromosome/combination is created, its *fitness* is evaluated to determine how good it is in identifying possible failure conditions. The following equation is used:

$$fitness\,(combination) = 1 - \%tests$$

where %*tests* is the percentage of test cases in T that exercised the combination; the smaller the percentage the higher the fitness. Ultimately, the aim is to end up with a manageable set of combinations in which each combination has a fitness value $\geq (1 - M_{fail}/|T|)$, ie, each combination occurred in at most M_{fail} tests.

9.2.3 Population Generation

The population is a collection of candidate solutions, which will evolve into the final solution. The population is formed, one bit string at a time, by taking a probabilistically randomized subset of the union of execution profiles of all test cases in T, where each element in the union profile is included in the combination at a certain (small) probability.

9.2.4 Transformation Operator

The authors employ "fitness-based crossover"; its basic functioning resembles that of genetic heredity, where a new chromosome is produced as a result of combining two parent chromosomes and passing down properties from each onto the new child, always favoring the parent with the higher fitness. The adopted genetic algorithm is a steady-state one, implying that the transformation is applied across generations, in each generation creating a single new child which replaces another individual in the population. To conduct the crossover, two parents are randomly selected from the population, and the child generated is one containing program elements from both parents. To ensure improvement of the child's fitness, more elements are taken from the parent with higher fitness. That is, each bit in the child chromosome is set to be equal to the same bit as one of its parents, favoring the better-fitted one according to a set probability factor. In the end, the resulting child replaces the parent with the worse fitness.

9.2.5 Acceptance Criterion

The fitness of a chromosome is evaluated to make two decisions: whether it is fit enough to include in the general population once it is created, and whether it is fit enough to be part of the final solution.

9.2.6 Stopping Criterion

Finally, the end of the generational evolution is determined by the number of generations or iterations executed. Typically, as more generations are used, more combinations are encountered and more defects are likely to be covered.

9.2.7 Solution Set

At the conclusion of the genetic algorithm, the obtained solution set contains all the encountered combinations with "suitable" fitness values, ie, high-enough values. Also, all single elements (combinations of 1 element) with appropriate fitness values are forcefully included so as to ensure that all possible defect-revealing elements are part of the solution.

9.3 Experimental Work

The subject programs included: (a) the *JTidy* HTML syntax checker and pretty printer, version 3; and (b) the *NanoXML* XML parser, version 3. The test suite, failures, and defects for *JTidy* are described in Section 8. *NanoXML* was downloaded along with its test suite from the SIR repository (*sir.unl.edu*). The seeded faults were injected into a single version that failed 20 times due to 4 defects. Note that the proportions of failures were made relatively low in order to mimic real-life situations.

In the study the following program elements were profiled: basic blocks or statements (BB); basic block edges or branches (BBE); and def-use pairs (DUP). Next the genetic algorithm is applied to generate the following: a pool of BB_{comb}, a pool of BBE_{comb}, a pool of DUP_{comb}, and a pool of ALL_{comb}, where BB_{comb} is a combination of BBs, BBE_{comb} is a combination of BBEs, DUP_{comb} is a combination of DUPs, and ALL_{comb} is a combination of BBs, BBEs, and DUPs. The generated pools were used to apply the minimization algorithm described in Section 8. Note that the values of M_{fail} chosen for *JTidy* and *NanoXML* were 100 and 20, respectively.

9.3.1 Minimization Results

Table 10 presents the results for *JTidy*. For example, in the case of ALL_{comb}, 14.1% of the original test suite was needed to exercise all of the combinations exercised by the original test suite, and these tests revealed all the defects revealed by the original test suite. Note that Section 8 showed that coverage of slice pairs (*SliceP*) performed better than coverage of BB, BBE, and DUP; this is why we are including the results of *SliceP* here for comparison. Also, note that the data shown were obtained by averaging the results of 1000

Table 10 Test Suite Minimization Results for *JTidy* (1000 Tests, 47 Failures, and 8 Defects)

Profile Type	# Tests Selected	% Tests Selected	# Failures Selected	% Failures Selected	# Defects Revealed	% Defects Revealed
BB	53.0	**5.3**	9.44	20.1	4.4	**55.0**
BB$_{comb}$	95.7	**9.6**	16.2	34.4	5.2	**65.6**
BBE	65.1	**6.5**	13.1	27.8	6.3	**78.7**
BBE$_{comb}$	102.2	**10.2**	19.7	41.9	7.0	**87.5**
DUP	117.3	**11.7**	18.8	40.0	6.5	**81.2**
DUP$_{comb}$	141.3	**14.1**	22.0	46.8	7.0	**87.5**
ALL[a]	123.6	**12.4**	20.2	42.9	7.6	**94.8**
ALL$_{comb}$	141.1	**14.1**	22.5	47.8	8.0	**100.0**
SliceP[a]	267.3	**26.7**	30.0	63.8	8.0	**100.0**

[a]These data originated from Section 8.

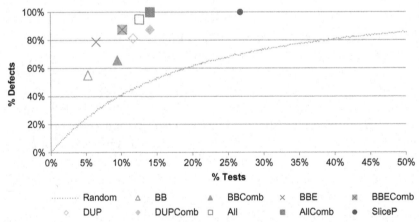

Fig. 13 Test suite minimization results for *JTidy* compared to random sampling.

different executions of the greedy selection algorithm, which explains why the columns showing the number of selected tests and the number of revealed defects contain fractions. Fig. 13 compares the various techniques to random sampling with respect to each technique's average effectiveness for revealing defects. The following observations are made from Fig. 13 and Table 10:

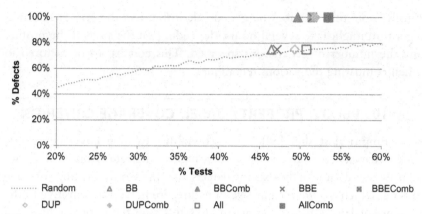

Fig. 14 Test suite minimization results for *NanoXML* compared to random sampling.

(1) All variations performed better than random sampling.

(2) BB_{comb} revealed 10.6% more defects than *BB* but selected 4.2% more tests.

(3) BBE_{comb} revealed 8.8% more defects than *BBE* but selected 3.7% more tests.

(4) DUP_{comb} revealed 6.3% more defects than *DUP* but selected 2.4% more tests.

(5) ALL_{comb} performed better than *SliceP*, since it: (a) revealed all defects, as *SliceP* did; (b) selected 12.6% less tests; and (c) cost less to profile.

Concerning observations (2), (3), and (4), the additional cost due to the selection of more tests might not be well justified, since it is apparent from Fig. 1 that the rate of improvement is no better than it is for random sampling. However, concerning observation (5), not only did ALL_{comb} perform better than *SliceP*, but it is considerably less costly since it took 90 s on average per test to generate its profiles (ie, *BBs*, *BBEs*, and *DUPs*), whereas it took 1200 s per test to generate the *SliceP* profiles (see Section 8).

Fig. 14 presents the results for *NanoXML* from which one can observe that:

(1) Variations not involving combinations (*BB, BBE, DUP, ALL*) did not perform any better than random sampling, whereas those involving combinations (*BB_{comb}, BBE_{comb}, DUP_{comb}, ALL_{comb}*) performed noticeably better.

(2) Variations that involved combinations revealed all the defects, but at relatively high cost, since over 50% of the tests were needed to be executed.

Finally, note that running the genetic algorithm and the greedy selection algorithm might take several hours, depending on the sizes of the profiles and the number of generations specified. This cost has to be factored in when comparing the various techniques.

10. PBCOV: PROPERTY-BASED COVERAGE CRITERION

Empirical studies [34] have shown that existing coverage criteria might characterize a given test suite as highly adequate, while it does not actually reveal some of the existing defects. In other words, existing coverage criteria, which are *structural* or *logic* in nature, are not always sensitive to the presence of defects. In an attempt to address this issue, the authors in Ref. [35] presented PBCOV, a new coverage approach that comprises a property-based coverage criterion, an associated metric, and a supporting tool.

Given a program with properties therein, static analysis techniques, such as model checking, leverage formal properties to find defects. PBCOV is a dynamic analysis technique that also leverages properties and is characterized by the following: (a) it considers the state space of first-order logic properties as the test requirements to be covered; (b) it uses logic synthesis to compute the state space; and (c) it is practical, ie, computable, because it considers an overapproximation of the reachable state space using a cut-based abstraction.

PBCOV was evaluated using programs with test suites comprising passing and failing test cases. First, coverage metrics values were computed for PBCOV and structural criteria using the full test suites. Second, in order to quantify the sensitivity of the metrics to the absence of failing test cases, the values for all considered metrics using only the passing test cases were computed. In most cases, the structural metrics exhibited little or no decrease in their values, while the PBCOV metrics showed a considerable decrease. This suggests that PBCOV is more sensitive to the absence of failing test cases; ie, it is more effective at characterizing test suite adequacy to detect defects and at revealing deficiencies in test suites.

10.1 Motivating Example

To illustrate the advantages of covering properties as opposed to structural elements, a faulty implementation of selection sort [36] is used, shown in Fig. 15. The function "sort()" takes as input an array "a" of size "n"; "current" and "j" are the iterators of the outer and inner loops, respectively; "lowestindex" holds the index of the minimum element so far in the array; and "temp" is used to perform the swap on lines 13–18. Line 9 has

```
 1 void sort ( int a[], int n) {        Test suite T = {
 2   int current, j, lowestindex, temp;      t₁ = ⟨1 2 3 4 5 6 7 8 9⟩,
 3                                            t₂ = ⟨9 8 7 6 5 4 3 2 1⟩,
 4   for ( current = 0; current < n-1; current++ ) {   t₃ = ⟨2 1 3 4 5 6 7 8 9⟩,
 5     // find the minimum                    t₄ = ⟨9 2 3 4 5 6 7 1⟩,
 6     lowestindex = current;                 t₅ = ⟨9 8 7 4 5 6 7 8 3 2 1⟩,
 7     j = current+1;                         t₆ = ⟨1 2⟩,
 8     while ( j < n ) {                      t₇ = ⟨1⟩,
 9       if ( a[j] < a[current] )             t₈ = ⟨⟩ }
10         lowestindex = j;
11       j++;                              After sort A = {
12     }                                      a₁ = ⟨1 2 3 4 5 6 7 8 9 ⟩,
13     // swap                                a₂ = ⟨1 2 3 4 5 6 7 8 9 ⟩,
14     if ( lowestindex != current ) {        a₃ = ⟨1 2 3 4 5 6 7 8 9 ⟩,
15       temp = a[current];                   a₄ = ⟨1 2 3 4 5 6 7 9 ⟩,
16       a[current] = a[lowestindex];         a₅ = ⟨1 2 3 4 5 6 7 7 8 8 9 ⟩,
17       a[lowestindex] = temp;               a₆ = ⟨1 2 ⟩,
18     } } }                                  a₇ = ⟨1 ⟩,
19 // fix: replace Line 9 with "if (a[j] < a[lowestindex])"   a₈ = ⟨⟩ }
```

Fig. 15 Motivating example for PBCOV.

a defect as it erroneously compares "a[j]" to "a[current]" as opposed to "a [lowestindex]"; thus, the inner loop does not always select the minimum. But due to coincidental correctness [37,38] the defect at line 9 could be exercised without leading to failure. For example, the test cases in test suite T shown in Fig. 15 result in the sorted arrays in A of which none of them leads to failure. T apparently seems reasonable as it consists of nonsorted arrays of different sizes, a sorted array t_1, a reverse-sorted array t_2, and test cases that test boundary conditions such as t_7 and t_8.

The authors computed the structural coverage metrics resulting from executing T using GCOV and ATAC. GCOV computes four coverage metrics, the percentage of executed statements, executed branches, branches taken at least once, and invoked functions. ATAC measures basic block coverage, predicate coverage, and two forms of def-use coverage, namely, C-use and P-use coverage. A C-use is a use of the variable in a computation such as an arithmetic expression, and a P-use is a use of the variable in a predicate expression that evaluates to a Boolean value. The C-use measure ensures that there is at least one path between the definition and a computational use of a variable. The P-use measure ensures that there is at least one path between the definition of the variable and both the *true* and *false* valuations of a predicate contain the variable [39].

T achieves full C-use coverage except for one infeasible def-use pair consisting of the definition "lowestindex = current" on line 6 and the use of "lowestindex" in "a[current] = a[lowestindex]" on line 16. This def-use pair is not feasible because the execution of the use is in contradiction with the "if" condition predicate "lowestindex != current" on line 14. T also achieves full P-use coverage except for three infeasible P-use pairs. The first is the definition "j = current + 1" on line 7 and the "false" value of the loop predicate "j < n" on line 8. This is infeasible since current is bounded by "current < n-1" on line 4. The second infeasible pair is the definition "lowestindex = current" on line 6 and the *true* value of predicate "lowestindex != current" on line 14. The last infeasible pair is the definition "lowestindex = j" on line 10 and the *false* value of the predicate "lowestindex != current" on line 14. This is infeasible since "j" is guaranteed to be different than "current" as it starts at "current+1" on line 7 and only gets incremented later. T achieves full coverage for all the other GCOV and ATAC metrics. One could conclude that T is a deficient test suite since it attained full coverage using traditional structural techniques, which motivates the work on property-based coverage.

The user could introduce a property P in "sort()" specifying that at the end of execution every two arbitrary neighboring elements $a[k]$ and $a[k+1]$ within the bounds of the array must be in order:

$$P = forall\, k,\ (0 \leq k) \wedge (k < n - 1) \rightarrow a[k] \leq a[k+1]$$

where P has three atomic predicate terms $p_1 = (0 \leq k)$, $p_2 = (k < n - 1)$ and $p_3 = (a[k] \leq a[k+1])$, ie, $P = p_1 \wedge p_2 \rightarrow p_3$.

To enable the user to annotate code with properties, PBCOV provides the macro PBCOV_ASSERT. At line 19, the user could then add the following code:

```
for (int k= 0; k < n-1; k++) {
    PBCOV_ASSERT ( !(k >= 0 && k < n) || (a[k+1] >= a[k]) );
}
```

Note how a loop is needed to simulate the *forall* quantifier in P, and the implication operator was substituted by its C language equivalent, ie, $p_1 \wedge p_2 \rightarrow p_3$ is substituted by $\neg(p_1 \wedge p_2) \vee p_3$.

The state space of P comprises eight states, seven of which satisfy P, and one {110} does not. In this failing state, k is in the correct range and satisfies $(p_1 \wedge p_2)$, but at least two of the array entries are not in order, thus violating p_3.

PBCOV determines that the states {001}, {011}, {101}, {000}, {010}, and {100} are infeasible, and consequently, the reachable state space only includes {111} where the property P passes, and {110} where it fails.

However, the test cases in T cover only one of the two reachable states; specifically, test cases t_1 through t_6 cover state {111} and test cases t_7 and t_8

do not exercise P and thus do not cover any states. This deems T as deficient since it does not cover $\{110\}$.

In addition, PBCOV automatically generates the test case $= \langle 1, 0, -1, 0 \rangle$ as an input that satisfies the state $\{110\}$. This test case reveals the bug as it results in the erroneous output $= \langle 0, -1, 0, 1 \rangle$ and should therefore be included in test suite T.

10.2 PBCOV Design and Implementation

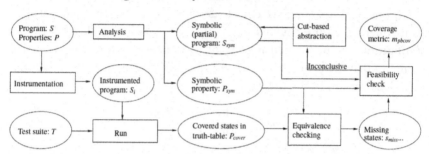

The diagram above illustrates the flow of PBCOV computation. Given a program S and a set of properties P, PBCOV computes S_i an instrumented version of S, S_{sym} a partial symbolic representation of S, and P_{sym} a symbolic representation of P. PBCOV runs the test suite T against S_i and computes P_{cover} the set of covered states. PBCOV uses equivalence checking techniques in model checking tools such as ABC [40] to compute the difference between P_{sym} and P_{cover}. Then PBCOV checks the feasibility of each s_{miss} state from $P_{sym} - P_{cover}$ against $S_{sym} \Rightarrow P_{sym}$ using a satisfiability modulo theory solver such as Yices [41]. If the solver returns an inconclusive result, then PBCOV over approximates S_{sym} by using a min–cut-based program slicing technique. The overapproximation computes a cut in the control flow diagram corresponding to S_{sym} and considers the variables crossing the cut as free variables. This is an overapproximation since the free variables may assume values that are not feasible. In case the solver returns a satisfiable result, the result could be used as an additional test case and s_{miss} is included in the metric. In case the solver returns an unsatisfiable result, then s_{miss} is deemed unreachable and is not used in the denominator of the metric.

PBCOV uses CREST [42] to analyze and instrument S, it computes n_{cov}^{true} to be the number of covered states that evaluate P to true, n_{cov}^{false} to be the number of covered states that evaluate P to false. It also computes n_{feas}^{true} and n_{cov}^{false} to be the number of feasible states that set P to *true* and *false*, respectively. PBCOV defines the metric to be:

$$m_{pbcov} = \frac{\log\left(1 + n_{cov}^{true} + n_{cov}^{false}\right)}{\log\left(1 + n_{feas}^{true} + n_{feas}^{false}\right)}$$

PBCOV uses the logarithmic scale to provide numbers that are in the same order of typical coverage techniques. Typically an overapproximation of the feasible state space is exponential in nature, while the number of covered states is polynomial in nature since test suites must be designed such that testing terminates within reasonable time limits.

In practice, designers fix defects denoted by a nonzero value of n_{cov}^{false}. Consequently, all the covered states after fixing defects evaluate P to *true*. Verification engineers then may want to estimate the property coverage assuming that the property is true, for that PBCOV defines an optimistic/confident version of the metric:

$$m_{pbcov}^{con} = \frac{\log\left(1 + n_{cov}^{true}\right)}{\log\left(1 + n_{feas}^{true}\right)}$$

The difference between the confident and the actual PBCOV metrics, $m_{pbcov} - m_{pbcov}^{con}$, quantifies the level of confidence of a test engineer when he or she deems a test suite to be adequate. A large difference means that he or she is too confident. The two metrics are good indicators in programs where reachability analysis works well and concludes on significant cuts of the program. However, the denominator grows exponentially where the reachability analysis does not conclude except on small parts of the program, and thus the magnitude values of the metrics may mislead the user to doubt the test suite. In such cases, programmers should not use values of m_{pbcov} as absolute indicators; rather they should consider them relative to other instances of m_{pbcov} computed with different test suites.

10.3 Experimental Results

The authors applied PBCOV along with several structural coverage techniques to five programs with property annotations. The programs are TCAS, Red Black Binary Search Tree (RBBST), Linked List (LL), Memory Manager (MMAN), and GZIP. Each program is associated with a test suite and is seeded with a number of defects that are in general detectable by the test suite. In total, the authors worked with 90 versions of the programs with seeded defects. In order to evaluate PBCOV at detecting test suite adequacy for detecting defects versus other structural coverage metric, the authors split each test suite T into two disjoint sets T_{pass} and T_{fail}, where T_{pass} includes all test cases that pass (do not cause a crash and matches the program oracles) and T_{fail} includes all test cases that fail (either cause a crash or does not match the oracles). Then they computed the percentage decrease in coverage for each coverage metric. The authors used GCOV and ATAC to compute the structural coverage results.

They distinguished the following categories:

Category 1: In 13 of the 90 versions, PBCOV and other coverage metrics showed no percentage decrease. The authors refined the properties to refer to variables involved in the defects, and then the PBCOV metric showed a significant decrease for 10 of the 13 versions. This shows that PBCOV's quality can be enhanced by enhancing the properties, while that is not possible for the other techniques.

Category 2: In 19 versions, PBCOV showed significant decrease, while the other coverage metrics showed no change at all. This shows a serious problem in the effectiveness of structural coverage metrics at detecting the adequacy of a test suite.

Category 3: In 8 versions, PBCOV showed a significant decrease, while some coverage metrics showed a little decrease. Similar to category 2, this shows the utility of PBCOV to highlight the deficiency in the test suite when other metrics show a little change.

Category 4: In 17 versions, structural coverage metrics showed a significant decrease. PBCOV also showed a significant decrease and showed more sensitivity in most cases.

Category 5: In 4 versions, structural coverage metrics showed a little decrease, while PBCOV showed no change at all. However, for these versions T_{pass} already evaluates P to false which prompts the verification engineers to fix the defect before looking at the coverage results. T_{pass} contains test cases that cause the program to compute a wrong result but never display it, so the test case passes the oracle check; however, it fails the property P. A refinement of T_{pass} and T_{fail} to respect the property also would render this category empty.

Category 6: It contains 29 versions where no structural or PBCOV change occurred but where T_{pass} violated the properties, which is sufficient to alarm the test engineer. These 29 versions show the utility of property annotations to uncover defects.

In general, when properties exist, PBCOV is likely to perform better than GCOV and ATAC. In most cases, the structural coverage elements behave similarly; this is well explained by the subsumption relationship between them and by the relative maturity of the used test suites.

The main threat to PBCOV is that it requires programs to be annotated with properties. In the absence of meaningful properties, which is typical in software programs, PBCOV is not applicable.

In the presence of properties, PBCOV depends on the quality of the properties. Also the overapproximation of the state space provides no tight bound to give the testing engineer a feeling of being done with testing.

11. UCov: USER-DEFINED COVERAGE CRITERION

The goal of regression testing is to ensure that the behavior of existing code, believed correct by previous testing, is not altered by new program changes. The authors in Refs. [43,44] argue that the primary focus of regression testing should be on code associated with: (a) earlier bug fixes; and (b) particular application scenarios considered to be important by the developer or the tester. Since existing coverage criteria do not enable such focus, eg, 100% branch coverage does not guarantee that a given bug fix is exercised or a given application scenario is tested; they stress the need for a new and complementary coverage criterion in which *the user can define* a *test requirement characterizing a given behavior to be covered* as opposed to choosing from a pool of predefined and generic program elements.

The authors propose this new methodology and call it *UCov* wherein a test requirement is an execution pattern of program elements, and possibly predicates, that a test case must satisfy or cover. The proposed criterion is not meant to replace existing criteria but to complement them as it focuses the testing on important code patterns that could go untested otherwise.

UCov supports *test case intent verification*. For example, following a bug fix, the testing team may augment the regression test suite with the test case that revealed the bug. Evidently, this new test case induces an execution pattern associated with the bug; however, it might become obsolete due to code modifications not related to the bug. But *UCov*, based on the test case and a user-defined test requirement characterizing the bug, would:

(a) Detect whether the test requirement was satisfied or not.

(b) Determine whether test case intent verification passed or failed.

(c) Deem the test suite deficient in case test intent verification failed, thus suggesting that a new test case that satisfies the requirement needs to be generated.

It is also worth mentioning that the approach paves the way for *test case intent preservation*. For example, in the scenario above, a failed verification could be followed by automated test case generation whose aim is to satisfy the user-defined test requirement and thus *preserve* the intent of the test case.

Developers and testers leverage *use case scenarios* when designing test cases. These use case scenarios develop into initial test suites and program implementations. During maintenance, the introduction of new features results in augmenting the test suites with test cases that cover the added features and associated code modifications. The same applies to reported bugs and corresponding fixes. Intuitively, *UCov* documents the relation between the test cases and the corresponding code modifications in a manner that enables test case intent verification and preservation. Currently, the documentation of that relation often exists in the form of modification request records in source control repositories. *UCov* provides an Eclipse plugin, called *TRSpec*, to allow the user to express test case intent, ie, to specify user-defined test requirements using a friendly graphical interface.

At first, it might appear that *UCov* is simply meant to help cover more complex test requirements comprising some patterns or combinations of existing program elements. But in fact, its main goal is to cover *behaviors* as opposed to generic structural program elements, and to couple tests with intents to be verified and preserved.

The main advantages of *UCov* to the software maintenance process are described below:

- In *UCov*, a test case *t* that was coupled with a bug fix, a feature, or some scenario of interest to the tester/developer, is intended to verify an expected (correct) behavior of the application. In case *t* becomes obsolete, that expected behavior would go unverified, but due to *UCov* the tester will learn that *t* needs to be replaced.
- Evidently, even full coverage achieved by existing structural coverage criteria does not establish that all (or any) of the scenarios of a given algorithm are tested. Testers and/or developers could couple each scenario of an algorithm with a test case, thus relying on *UCov* to ensure coverage of these scenarios. This enables *validation testing* whose aim is to exercise the functionality of the *SUT*.
- *A bug fix could become faulty due to other code changes* (ie, a bug was introduced in the bug fix). *UCov* can detect that the test requirement associated with the bug fix is not satisfied, which calls for revisiting the bug fix and test suite.
- *Bug resurrection happens when faulty code that was fixed, gets introduced again.* Typically, this might happen due to the uncoordinated access of a file in a source control system by more than one developer. *UCov* ensures the coverage of the test requirement associated with the bug fix and thus uncovers the resurrecting bug. Without *UCov*, resurrecting bugs might escape typical structural coverage-based testing.

The authors in Refs. [43,44] implemented this methodology for the Java platform in the following tool set:

(a) *TRSpec*, an Eclipse plugin that enables users to easily define test requirements.

(b) *TRCheck*, a tool that checks whether the test requirements are satisfied (during test suite execution).

(c) *TRMigrate*, a tool that migrates test requirements to subsequent versions of a given program.

Next, we provide definitions and notation for specifying test requirements. Then we motivate the need for *UCov* by walking through three examples.

11.1 Definitions and Notation

This section provides definitions for entities relevant to *UCov*, and notation for specifying test requirements.

Definition—A *basic test requirement* (*btr*) is a logical expression over a set of program elements and logical operators such as negation ($\neg$), conjunction ($\wedge$), and disjunction ($\vee$). The semantics of a *btr* describe an execution of the program elements. For example, the *btr* $[(s_1 \vee b_1) \wedge (\neg dup_1)]_{btr}$ involves the set of program elements $\{s_1, b_1, dup_1\}$ and is satisfied if: (a) statement s_1 or branch b_1 did execute and (b) definition-use pair dup_1 did not execute.

Definition—A *test requirement* describes an execution pattern of program elements and possibly predicates that a *test case must satisfy* or cover. It is a *basic test requirement*, a *conditional test requirement*, a *sequential test requirement* (defined below), or a *repeated test requirement*.

- **Definition**—A *conditional test requirement* (*ctr*) is a test requirement comprising a test requirement *tr*, and a predicate *p* specifying a state of some program variables. For a conditional test requirement to be satisfied, *tr* should be satisfied, and *p* should evaluate to *true* immediately after. For example, the conditional test requirement $[[s_1 \wedge b_1]_{btr}, x > y]_{ctr}$ requires that statement s_1 and branch b_1 be executed and, when that happens, *x* be strictly greater than *y*.

- **Definition**—A *sequential test requirement* (*str*) is a test requirement composed of a sequence of at least two test requirements that must be satisfied one after the other. For example, the sequential test requirement $[<[b_1]_{btr}, [b_2]_{btr}, [b_3 \vee s_1]_{btr}>]_{str}$ requires that branches b_1 and b_2 be sequentially executed, followed by b_3 or s_1.

- **Definition**—A *repeated test requirement* (*rtr*) is a test requirement comprising a test requirement *tr*, and a range indicating the number of times it should be repeated. For example, the repeated test requirement $[[s_1 \wedge b_1]_{btr}, 5, 1000]_{rtr}$ requires that statement s_1 and branch b_1 be executed at least 5 times and at most 1000 times. In case one or both of the bounds do not matter, a *"don't care"* symbol could be specified; eg, $[[s_1]_{btr}, 100, \_]_{rtr}$ requires that statement s_1 be executed at least 100 times.

```
boolean terminateEmployee(int averageSales, int salary)
```

```
// P1
    int raise = 0;
    if (averageSales >= 1000000) {
        raise = 30000;
    } else if (averageSales >= 100000) {
        raise = 10000;
    } else if (averageSales >= 10000) {
        raise = 1000;
    }
    salary = salary + raise;

    //Bug: should be if (salary > 200000)
s1:    if (salary >= 200000) {
s2:        return true;
       } else {
s3:    return false; }
```

```
// P2
    int raise = 0;
    if (averageSales >= 1000000) {
        raise = 30000;
    } else if (averageSales >= 100000) {
        raise = 10000;
    } else if (averageSales >= 10000) {
        raise = 1000;
    }
    salary = salary + raise;

    //Bug is fixed
s1:    if (salary > 200000) {
s2:        return true;
       } else {
s3:        return false;    }
```

```
// P3
    if (averageSales > 3000000)
        return false; // Added code
    if (averageSales < 1000)
        return true; // Added code
    int raise = 0;
    if (averageSales >= 1000000) {
        raise = 30000;
    } else if (averageSales >= 100000) {
        raise = 10000;
    } else if (averageSales >= 10000) {
        raise = 1000;
    }
    salary = salary + raise;

s1:    if (salary > 200000) {
s2:        return true;
       } else {
s3:        return false;}
```

```
// P4
    if (averageSales > 3000000)
        return false;
    if(averageSales < 1000)
        return true;
    int raise = 0;
    if (averageSales >= 1000000) {
        raise = 30000;
    } else if (averageSales >= 100000) {
        raise = 10000;
    } else if (averageSales >= 10000) {
        raise = 1000;
    }
    salary = salary + raise;

s1:    if (salary >= 200000) { // Resurrected bug
s2:        return true;
       } else {
s3:        return false;}
```

11.2 Motivation

The premise behind *UCov* is that some tests are more important than others, and that current coverage criteria are not well suited to making sure that important tests not only are present but also continue to satisfy their intended function as code evolves. We now walk through three examples motivating *UCov*. The first demonstrates a case involving a bug fix, and the other two involve scenarios of significance.

11.2.1 Example 1—Testing a Bug Fix

Consider a program P_1, an associated test suite T_1, and a reported bug that was revealed by t_{bug}, a test case not present in T_1. The development team fixes the bug to produce P_2 and couples t_{bug} with a test requirement that characterizes the bug execution. The testing team augments T_1 with t_{bug} to form T_2, the regression test suite for P_2. Subsequently, P_2 is modified to add a feature or to refactor the code, thus resulting in P_3. Assume that the modification renders t_{bug} obsolete as it ceases to satisfy its test requirement. Consequently, T_2 becomes inadequate, which calls for replacing t_{bug} with a new test case.

As a concrete example, consider the function *boolean terminateEmployee(int averageSales, int salary)* which determines whether an employee should be terminated or not as follows: (a) it computes the next annual raise based on the average sales amount; (b) computes the new salary including the raise; and (c) recommends termination if the new salary exceeds some threshold (hardcoded to $200,000).

A faulty implementation P_1 of *terminateEmployee()* is shown below. The bug is in statement s_1 which induces a failure when the computed salary is exactly 200000. An example failing test case would be t_{bug}:{(4000000, 170000), false}, where *averageSales* is 4000000, current *salary* is 170000, and the return value is *true* (expected to be *false*). Also, consider test suite $T=\{t_1, t_2, t_3, t_{bug}\}$, where t_1:{(1500000, 100000), false}, t_2:{(130000, 50000), false}, and t_3:{(11000, 35000), false}. Note how T achieves full statement coverage and contains t_{bug} as the only failing test case.

Due to t_{bug} the developers fix the bug in P_2, and couple t_{bug} with a test requirement that characterizes the bug execution, specifically, t_{bug} *is coupled* with $tr_{bug} = [<[[s_1]_{btr}, salary == 200000]_{ctr}, [s_3]_{btr}>]_{str}$ (as one possibility). Meaning, in order for the intent of tr_{bug} to be preserved, salary should have a value of 200,000 at s_1, and s_3 should be executed following it.

Now assume that due to requirements changes, P_2 was modified to yield P_3. Particularly, two conditional statements were added at the beginning of the function to satisfy the following requirements: (1) if the average sales amount was exceptionally high, do not terminate the employee no matter how high the salary is; and (2) if the average sales amount was exceptionally low, terminate the employee no matter how low the salary is.

These changes have no effect on the execution of t_1, t_2, or t_3, but will render t_{bug} obsolete. That is, the intent of t_{bug} is not preserved in P_3 as tr_{bug} is not satisfied anymore. To remedy this problem, which would be alerted by $UCov$, the testing team replaces t_{bug} with t_{bug}':{(2000000, 170000), false} which satisfies $tr_{bug} = [<[[s_1]_{btr}, \ salary == 200000]_{ctr}, \ [s_3]_{btr}>]_{str}$. Consequently, the updated test suite becomes $T = \{t_1, t_2, t_3, t_{bug}'\}$.

Furthermore, assume that the bug resurrected in P_4, which is not very uncommon in practice. Note how t_{bug}' will reveal the bug in P_4. Whereas given a test suite that achieves full coverage will not necessarily do so. For example, test suite $T' = \{t_1, t_2, t_3, t_4, t_5\}$ exhibits 100% statement/branch coverage but does not reveal the bug in P_4, where t_1:{(1500000, 180000), true}, t_2:{(130000, 50000), false}, t_3:{(11000, 35000), false}, t_4: {(5000000, 150000), false}, and t_5:{(900, 20000), false}.

Finally, one may argue that to verify that the intent of a test case is satisfied it suffices to check whether its expected output is observed. This does not work in the above example since executing P_3 with t_{bug}:{(4000000, 170000), false} does yield the correct output, while the bug fix is not exercised.

11.2.2 Example 2—Testing Scenarios of an Algorithm

Typically, algorithms are presented while stressing the prime scenarios they support, which we believe should all be tested for quality assurance. Noting that even full coverage achieved by existing structural coverage criteria does not establish that all (or any) of the scenarios of an algorithm are tested, we advocate $UCov$ as an effective solution to this task. Intuitively, each documented scenario (or case) associated with the algorithm describes at least one test requirement (execution pattern) that should be coupled with designated test cases. We illustrate the usage of $UCov$ in testing the algorithm for deleting a node in a binary search tree.

The algorithm in Fig. 16 presented in Ref. [45] considers four cases concerning the node z to be deleted:

Case 1: If z has no children, then it is replaced by NIL.

Case 2: If z has only one child, then it is replaced by that child.

Case 3: If z has two children, then it is replaced by its successor, which is the leftmost node in the subtree rooted at the right child of z. In this case, the successor of z (say y) has no right child. That is, y would be a leaf and

```
BST-DELETE(T, z)
Input: Binary Search Tree (T), pointer to the node to be deleted (z)
Output: Binary Search Tree (T') obtained from T by deleting z
1.     if left[z] = NIL or right[z] = NIL
2.         then y ← z
3.     else y ← TREE-SUCCESSOR(z)

4.     if left[y] ≠ NIL
5.         then x ← left[y]
6.     else x ← right[y]

7.     if x ≠ NIL
8.         then p[x] ← p[y]

9.     if p[y] = NIL
10.        then root[T] ← x
11.    else if y = left[p[y]]
12.        then left[p[y]] ← x
13.    else right[p[y]] ← x

14.    if y ≠ z
15.        then key[z]← key[y]
16.            copy y's satellite data into z
```

Fig. 16 Pseudo-code for deleting a node in a BST.

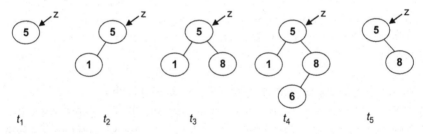

t_1 t_2 t_3 t_4 t_5

Fig. 17 Test suite $T=\{t_1, t_2, t_3, t_4, t_5\}$.

thus deleting z would be achieved by replacing the contents of z by those of y and replacing y with NIL.

Case 4: Similar to *Case3*, z has two children and is replaced by its successor. However, here y has a right child, and the contents of z are replaced by those of y but instead of replacing y with NIL, it is replaced by its right child.

Fig. 17 depicts a test suite T comprising five test cases t_1, t_2, t_3, t_4, and t_5. Table 11 details the individual and cumulative branch coverage information for each of the test cases. As shown, T achieves 100% branch coverage. Although not obvious in Table 11, T also satisfies MC/DC coverage [46].

The test requirements associated with each of the algorithm's scenarios are also shown at the bottom of Table 11, along with T's coverage

Table 11 Coverage Information for Test Suite T

		t_1	t_2	t_3	t_4	t_5	T
Branches	S1 → S2	✓	✓	✗	✗	✓	✓
	S1 → S3	✗	✗	✓	✓	✗	✓
	S4 → S5	✗	✓	✗	✗	✗	✓
	S4 → S6	✓	✗	✓	✓	✓	✓
	S7 → S8	✗	✓	✗	✗	✓	✓
	S7 → S9	✓	✗	✓	✓	✗	✓
	S9 → S10	✓	✓	✗	✗	✓	✓
	S9 → S11	✗	✗	✓	✓	✗	✓
	S11 → S12	✗	✗	✗	✓	✗	✓
	S11 → S13	✗	✗	✓	✗	✗	✓
	S14 → S15	✗	✗	✓	✓	✗	✓
	S14 → END	✓	✓	✗	✗	✓	✓
Prime Scenarios	Execution Patterns (TR)						
Case 1	$[<[s_2]_{btr}, [s_6]_{btr}, [[s_7]_{btr}, x==NIL]_{ctr}>]_{str}$	✓	✗	✗	✗	✗	✓
Case 2	$[<[s_2]_{btr}, [s_8]_{btr}>]_{str}$	✗	✓	✗	✗	✓	✓
Case 3	$[<[s_3]_{btr}, [s_6]_{btr}, [[s_7]_{btr}, x==NIL]_{ctr}>]_{str}$	✗	✗	✓	✓	✗	✓
Case 4	$[<[s_3]_{btr}, [s_6]_{btr}, [s_8]_{btr}>]_{str}$	✗	✗	✗	✗	✗	✗

information. Test case t_1 covers the test requirement of *Case 1*. Test cases t_2 and t_5 satisfy the test requirement of *Case 2*. And both t_3 and t_4 cover the test requirement of *Case 3*, whereas *Case 4* is left untested; ie, none of the tests cover test requirement $[<[s_3]_{btr}, [s_6]_{btr}, [s_8]_{btr}>]_{str}$.

This example demonstrates how applying our coverage criterion would deem test suite T deficient despite the fact that it satisfied full branch coverage and the stronger MC/DC coverage. In order to test all four scenarios using *UCov*, the user would: (1) specify their four respective test requirements shown at the bottom of Table 1; and (2) design at least one test case that covers it for each test requirement.

One may argue that refactoring the code in Fig. 16 into four methods each corresponding to one of the four cases at hand would allow simple coverage criteria to reveal whether some scenario went untested. This is true, but unfortunately it cannot be assumed that developers will always break down their code with scenarios in mind. Also, recall that the pseudo-code in Fig. 16 was drawn from a highly regarded source which makes it likely that a developer would implement it as is.

11.2.3 Example 2—Testing Inactive Clauses

This example demonstrates the utility of *UCov* in testing a scenario involving inactive clauses. Note that *UCov* is not designed to specifically test inactive clauses, but this example is meant to show the flexibility and power of *UCov*.

The scenario discussed here is described in Ref. [1]. Consider the function *bool reset()* that is designed to control the shutdown system in a nuclear reactor:

```
boolean reset()
{
s1:    boolean result = false;
s2:    if (override || valveClosed)
s3:             result = true;
s4:    return result;
}
```

When the system is in *"override"* mode, the state of a particular valve (*"open"* vs *"closed"*) should not affect the decision to reset the system. A conservative approach would require testing *reset()* in override mode for both positions of the valve. Using *UCov*, this could be achieved by satisfying the following two test requirements:

$[[s_4]_{btr}, override==true \wedge valveClosed==true \wedge result==true]_{ctr}$

$[[s_4]_{btr}, override==true \wedge valveClosed==false \wedge result==true]_{ctr}$

On the other hand, each of the test suites below satisfies some established coverage criterion without actually checking whether *valveClosed* is inactive:

(1) Statement and branch coverage are both satisfied by:

```
{ (override=true, valveClosed=false, result=true),
(override=false, valveClosed=false, result=false) }
```

(2) Clause coverage is satisfied by:

```
{ (override=true, valveClosed=true, result=true),
(override=false, valveClosed=false, result=false) }
```

(3) MC/DC coverage is satisfied by:

```
{ (override=true, valveClosed=false, result=true),
(override=false, valveClosed=false, result=false),
(override=false, valveClosed=true, result=true) }
```

Of course combinatorial coverage does test whether clause *valveClosed* is inactive, but it requires four tests as opposed to two.

12. CONCLUSION

Early coverage-based software testing techniques involved basic test requirements such as functions, statements, branches, and predicates, whereas recent techniques involved (1) test requirements that are complex code constructs such as paths, program dependences, and information flows; or (2) test requirements that are not necessarily code constructs such as program properties, and user-defined test requirements. This chapter described these two generations of techniques and compared them when applicable. It also provided preliminary background and definitions and described relevant work such as approaches to execution profiling.

Most practitioners rely solely on code coverage to assess the quality of software. However, we recognize several limitations to such strategy:

(1) Coverage techniques are inherently unable to reveal faults that are due to missing conditionals or omitted code.

(2) Even 100% coverage of the most complex test requirements is no guarantee that the code is bug free. This is the case because test requirements are not likely to characterize all program behaviors or use cases.

(3) Coverage is a useful tool for finding untested parts of the code, but it is of little use as a numeric statement of how good your tests are; as asserted by Fowler [47]. That is, even though low levels of coverage (say below 50%) are a sign of trouble, high levels do not necessarily mean that the software is of high quality.

(4) Most organizations require a target level of coverage, which might backfire. This was argued by Marick [48]:

(a) *"The problem with this approach is that people optimize their performance according to how they're measured. You can get 85% coverage by looking at the coverage conditions, picking the ones that seem easiest to satisfy, writing quick tests for them, and iterating until done."* That is, testers might be implicitly encouraged to spend their precious time writing quick tests that increase coverage as opposed to writing tests that might reveal faults. In other words, targeting a level of coverage might distract the testers from developing test cases that really matter [47].

(b) In some organizations where the target level of coverage is at set point such as Marick's 85%, it was observed in Ref. [48] that a sizable number of testers achieved around 85% but not much more. This happened, not because these testers were unable to find additional tests that might increase coverage or reveal more faults, but because once they reached the required level, they stopped testing. The reason is they felt that their job was done [48].

(c) Keep in mind that setting a target level of coverage has a clear benefit as it gives the testers a point where they can stop testing, especially that testing is a pressing job that typically comes at the end of the time to market race. Since exhaustive testing is impossible and time to market is a very sensitive factor in the success of a software release, testers consider reaching a coverage target as a good stopping point for testing, which is otherwise undefined.

To finalize, the software testing community believes that the use of coverage criteria makes it more likely that faults are found and provides informal assurance of the reliability of the software. This is not a scientifically supported proposition, but it is the best out there [1]. On a more positive note, considering the emerging coverage criteria that complement existing structural coverage criteria, it appears that the path to formalizing the *science of testing* is getting clearer and shorter.

REFERENCES

[1] P. Ammann, J. Offutt, Introduction to Software Testing, first ed., Cambridge University Press, Cambridge, UK, 2008. ISBN-10: 0521880386; ISBN-13: 978-0521880381.
[2] P. Ammann, A. Jefferson Offutt, H. Huang, Coverage criteria for logical expressions, ISSRE (2003) 99–107.
[3] R. Abou-Assi, W. Masri, Identifying failure-correlated dependence chains, in: First International Workshop on Testing and Debugging, TeBug, Berlin, 2011.
[4] W. Masri, Fault localization based on information flow coverage, J. Softw. Test. Verif. Reliab. 20 (2) (2010) 121 147.
[5] W. Masri, A. Podgurski, D. Leon, An empirical study of test case filtering techniques based on exercising information flows, IEEE Trans. Softw. Eng. 33 (7) (2007) 454.
[6] W. Masri, Exploiting the empirical characteristics of program dependences for improved forward computation of dynamic slice, Emp. Softw. Eng. 13 (2008) 369–399.
[7] W. Masri, A. Podgurski, Algorithms and tool support for dynamic information flow analysis, Inf. Softw. Technol. 51 (2009) 395–404.
[8] W. Masri, H. Halabi, An algorithm for capturing variables dependences in test suites, J. Syst. Softw. 84 (7) (2011) 1171–1190.
[9] W. Masri, R. Abou Assi, M. El-Ghali, Generating profile-based signatures for online intrusion and failure detection, Inf. Softw. Technol. 56 (2) (2014) 238–251.
[10] W. Masri, J. Daou, R. Abou-Assi, State profiling of internal variables, in: Regression/ICST 2014, Cleveland, 2014.
[11] The Byte Code Engineering Library (BCEL), The Apache Jakarta Project, http://jakarta.apache.org/bcel. Apache Software Foundation 2003.
[12] ASM, http://asm.ow2.org/, last accessed January 2016.
[13] Pin, https://software.intel.com/en-us/articles/pin-a-dynamic-binary-instrumentation-tool, last accessed January 2016.
[14] T. Ball, J.R. Larus, Efficient path profiling, Proc. MICRO (1996) 46–57.
[15] T. Ball, J.R. Larus, Optimally profiling and tracing programs, ACM Trans. Program. Lang. Syst. 16 (4) (1994) 1319–1360.
[16] G. Fraser, A. Arcuri, EvoSuite: automatic test suite generation for object-oriented software, in: SIGSOFT FSE, 2011, pp. 416–419.

[17] J.C. King, Symbolic execution and program testing, Commun. ACM 19 (7) (1976) 385–394.

[18] K. Sen, D. Marinov, G. Agha, CUTE: a concolic unit testing engine for C, in: ESEC/ SIGSOFT FSE, 2005, pp. 263–272.

[19] P. Godefroid, P. de Halleux, A.V. Nori, S.K. Rajamani, W. Schulte, N. Tillmann, M.Y. Levin, Automating software testing using program analysis, IEEE Softw. (2008).

[20] B. Korel, A dynamic approach of test data generation, in: IEEE Conference on Software Maintenance, San Diego, 1990, pp. 311–317.

[21] B. Korel, Dynamic method of software test data generation, Softw. Test. Verif. Reliab. 2 (4) (1992) 203–213.

[22] P. Godefroid, M.Y. Levin, D.A. Molnar, SAGE: whitebox fuzzing for security testing, ACM Queue 10 (1) (2012) 20.

[23] P. Godefroid, N. Klarlund, K. Sen, DART: directed automated random testing, in: PLDI, 2005, pp. 213–223.

[24] N. Tillmann, J. de Halleux, PEX—white box test generation for .NET, Tests Proofs (2008).

[25] A.V. Nori, S.K. Rajamani, S.D. Tetali, A.V. Thakur, The YOGI project: software property checking via static analysis and testing, in: TACAS, 2009.

[26] T. Ball, S.K. Rajamani, Automatically validating temporal safety properties of interfaces, in: SPIN 2001, Lecture Notes on Computer Science (LNCS), 2001.

[27] C. Cadar, D. Dunbar, D.R. Engler, KLEE: unassisted and automatic generation of high-coverage tests for complex systems programs, in: OSDI, 2008, pp. 209–224.

[28] D.S. Hochbaum, Approximation Algorithms for NP-Hard Problems, PWS Publishing, Boston, MA, 1997.

[29] H. Agrawal, J. Horgan, Dynamic program slicing, SIGPLAN Notices 25 (6) (1990) 246–256.

[30] W. Masri, N. Nahas, A. Podgurski, Memoized forward computation of program slices, in: 17th IEEE International Symposium on Software Reliability Engineering (ISSRE 2006), Raleigh, NC, USA, 2006, pp. 23–32.

[31] J. Farjo, R. Abou Assi, W. Masri, Reducing execution profiles: techniques and benefits, Softw. Test. Verif. Reliab. 25 (2) (2015) 115–137.

[32] W. Masri, M. El-Ghali, Test case filtering and prioritization based on coverage of combinations of program elements, in: Seventh International Workshop on Dynamic Analysis, WODA, Chicago, IL, 2009.

[33] W. Masri, R. Abou-Assi, M. El-Ghali, N. Fatairi, An empirical study of the factors that reduce the effectiveness of coverage-based fault localization, in: International Workshop on Defects in Large Software Systems, DEFECTS, Chicago, IL, 2009.

[34] L. Inozemtseva, R. Holmes, Coverage is not strongly correlated with test suite effectiveness, in: ICSE, 2014, pp. 435–445.

[35] K. Fawaz, F.A. Zaraket, W. Masri, H. Harkous, PBCOV: a property-based coverage criterion, Softw. Qual. J. 23 (1) (2015) 171–202.

[36] A. Barr, Find the Bug: A Book of Incorrect Programs, Addison-Wesley Professional, 2004.

[37] W. Masri, R. Abou-Assi, Cleansing test suites from coincidental correctness to enhance fault-localization, in: Third International Conference on Software Testing, Verification and Validation, ICST, Paris, France, 2010.

[38] W. Masri, R. Abou Assi, Prevalence of coincidental correctness and mitigation of its impact on fault-localization, ACM Trans. Softw. Eng. Methodol. 23 (1) (2014) 8.

[39] S. Rapps, E.J. Weyuker, Data flow analysis techniques for test data selection, in: International Conference on Software Engineering, Los Alamitos, CA, USA, 1982, pp. 272–278.

[40] ABC, ABC: Berkeley Logic Synthesis and Verification Group. A System for Sequential Synthesis and Verification, 2007. http://www.eecs.berkeley.edu/alanmi/abc/release 70930.

[41] B. Dutertre, L.M.D. Moura, A fast linear-arithmetic solver for dpll(t), Comput. Aid. Verif. (2006) 81–94.

[42] J. Burnim, K. Sen, Heuristics for scalable dynamic test generation, in: International Conference on Automated Software Engineering, 2008, pp. 443–446.

[43] E. Shaccour, F.A. Zaraket, W. Masri, Coverage specification for test case intent preservation in regression suites, in: ICST Workshops, 2013, pp. 392–395.

[44] R.A. Assi, F.A. Zaraket, W. Masri, UCov: a user-defined coverage criterion for test case intent verification, CoRR (2014). abs/1407.3091.

[45] T. Cormen, C. Leiserson, R. Rivest, C. Stein, Introduction to Algorithms, third ed., The MIT Press, Boston, MA, USA, 2009. ISBN-10: 0262033844; ISBN-13: 978-0262033848.

[46] J. Joseph Chilenski, S.P. Miller, Applicability of modified condition/decision coverage to software testing, Softw. Eng. J. 9 (5) (1994) 193–200.

[47] M. Fowler, TestCoverage, http://martinfowler.com/bliki/TestCoverage.html, last accessed January 2016.

[48] B. Marick, How to misuse code coverage, 1999. http://www.exampler.com/testing-com/writings/coverage.pdf.

ABOUT THE AUTHORS

Wes Masri is an Associate Professor in the ECE Department at the American University of Beirut. His research interest is in software engineering, primarily in software testing and analysis. He received his PhD in Computer Engineering from Case Western Reserve University in 2005, M.S. from Penn State in 1988, and B.S. also from Case Western Reserve University in 1986. He also spent over 15 years in the U.S. software industry mainly as a software architect and developer. Some of the industries he was involved in include medical imaging, middleware, telecom, genomics, semiconductor, document imaging, and financial.

Fadi Zaraket is an Assistant Professor in the ECE Department at The American University of Beirut. He received his PhD in ECE from UT Austin in December 2007. He received his Masters and Bachelor degrees in CCE from The American University of Beirut in February 2001 and July 1996, respectively. He worked at IBM on logic verification and debugging tools between June 2001 and December 2008. He also worked at Sun Microsystems and Santa Cruz Operations on kernel development between April 1999 and June 2001.

AUTHOR INDEX

A

Abella, F., 22
Abou-Assi, R., 89, 110–111, 118, 124–125
Abraham, A., 22
Acharya, M., 61
Agha, G., 99–102
Agmon Ben-Yehuda, O., 13
Agrawal, H., 59, 62, 104
Aiken, A.S., 45
Ajila, S.A., 22
Akansu, A.N., 8
Akhlaghi, S., 61
Ali-Eldin, A., 8–9, 22
Almezen, H., 58
Alourani, A., 2–6, 12–23, 32–48
Amarasinghe, S., 46
Amato, N.M., 46
Ammann, P., 68, 80–82, 138, 140
Ammons, G., 35
Anderson, J.W., 47
Andrzejak, A., 19–20
Anido, R., 68
Ansel, J., 46
Arafeen, M., 63–64, 66–67
Arcuri, A., 98–99
Arlt, S., 70
Armbrust, M., 3, 17
Arul, M., 63–64
Assi, R.A., 130, 132
Avesani, P., 64
Avresky, D.R., 19

B

Bacigalupo, D., 22
Bai, X., 6
Balakrishnan, H., 22
Ball, T., 35, 93, 95, 97–98, 102–103
Barr, A., 124–125
Bates, S., 59
Bean, K., 8
Beatty, D., 32–33
Benatallah, B., 7, 12–14
Ben-Yehuda, M., 13
Bertolino, A., 68

Bianchini, R., 22
Bible, J., 58
Bigus, J., 22
Bikas, Md.A.N., 2–6, 12–23, 32–48
Blue, D., 69–70
Bobroff, N., 19
Bode, A., 19
Bodık, P., 22
Brace, K., 32–33
Brandić, I., 7, 12–14
Braud, R., 47
Brebner, P.C., 5, 13–14, 18–20
Breitgand, D., 8
Briand, L.C., 58–59, 61–62
Bryant, R.E., 32–33
Bryce, R., 65
Buford, J.F., 22
Burnim, J., 47, 127–128
Buyya, R., 4, 6–9, 17–20, 22

C

Cadar, C., 103
Calheiros, R.N., 8, 17–18, 22
Cao, Z., 22
Carlson, R., 64
Carrera, D., 8–9
Caşcaval, C., 47
Castillo, C., 19
Catal, C., 56, 64–65
Cavalli, A., 68
Chaisiri, S., 20–21
Chana, I., 22
Chandra, A., 22
Chang, E., 12–13
Chapin, N., 32
Charalambous, T., 22
Chattopadhyay, S., 45–46
Chen, B., 6
Chen, H., 4, 22
Chen, T., 47
Chen, T.Y., 68
Chen, Y., 58
Chen, Y.F., 57

SUBJECT INDEX

Note: Page numbers followed by "*f*" indicate figures, and "*t*" indicate tables.

CONTENTS OF VOLUMES IN THIS SERIES

157

Volume 94

Comparison of Security Models: Attack Graphs Versus Petri Nets
    STEVEN C. WHITE AND SAHRA SEDIGH SARVESTANI
A Survey on Zero-Knowledge Proofs
    LI FENG AND BRUCE MCMILLIN
Similarity of Private Keyword Search over Encrypted Document Collection
    YOUSEF ELMEHDWI, WEI JIANG, AND ALIREZA HURSON
Multiobjective Optimization for Software Refactoring and Evolution
    ALI OUNI, MAROUANE KESSENTINI, AND HOUARI SAHRAOUI

Volume 95

Automated Test Oracles: A Survey
    MAURO PEZZÈ AND CHENG ZHANG
Automated Extraction of GUI Models for Testing
    PEKKA AHO, TEEMU KANSTRÉN, TOMI RÄTY, AND JUHA RÖNING
Automated Test Oracles: State of the Art, Taxonomies, and Trends
    RAFAEL A.P. OLIVEIRA, UPULEE KANEWALA, AND PAULO A. NARDI
Anti-Pattern Detection: Methods, Challenges, and Open Issues
    FABIO PALOMBA, ANDREA DE LUCIA, GABRIELE BAVOTA, AND ROCCO OLIVETO
Classifying Problems into Complexity Classes
    WILLIAM GASARCH

Volume 96

An Overview of Selected Heterogeneous and Reconfigurable Architectures
    SAŠA STOJANOVIĆ, DRAGAN BOJIĆ, AND MIROSLAV BOJOVIĆ
Concurrency, Synchronization, and Speculation—The Dataflow Way
    KRISHNA KAVI, CHARLES SHELOR, AND DOMENICO PACE
Dataflow Computing in Extreme Performance Conditions
    DIEGO ORIATO, STEPHEN GIRDLESTONE, AND OSKAR MENCER
Sorting Networks on Maxeler Dataflow Supercomputing Systems
    ANTON KOS, VUKAŠIN RANKOVIĆ, AND SAŠO TOMAŽIČ
Dual Data Cache Systems: Architecture and Analysis
    ZIVOJIN SUSTRAN, GORAN RAKOCEVIC, AND VELJKO MILUTINOVIC

Volume 97

Comparing Reuse Strategies in Different Development Environments
    JULIA VARNELL-SARJEANT AND ANNELIESE AMSCHLER ANDREWS
Advances in Behavior Modeling
    ELLA ROUBTSOVA
Overview of Computational Approaches for Inference of MicroRNA-Mediated and Gene
Regulatory Networks
    BLAGOJ RISTEVSKI

Printed in the United States
By Bookmasters